FOREWORD

The most important and most misused element of menswear is that of fashion. Considering the confusion, claims and counterclaims about what is taking place in our field today, it would seem worthwhile to reflect on just what fashion really does mean.

With the changes going on in our world today, it is the culture that demands fashion. Any retailer, any manufacturer, any designer who is unaware of these changes will be, after a while, destroyed by the dated quality of his merchandise. Numerous examples could be cited of progressive manufacturers, designers and retailers who have been successful because they understand the dynamics of change and fashion. This success has occurred not only in the freaky world of alternate culture boutiques, but across the board from business suits to sportswear.

We have seen in the past few years a tremendous cultural change among men: there is a polarization between young and old, establishment and radicalism, conformity and individualism. We have often talked about how this has led, in our view, to the creation of three distinct fashion markets: Dominant, Middle and Alternate.

Thus, to ignore fashion in today's culture or to define it incorrectly are both mistakes. Instead, if you think of fashion as a constant, broad supply of new ideas stimulating the consumer to loosen up, to express pleasure in his clothes, to accept change, you will be in the right position to deal with today's world.

With all that in mind, how extraordinary to discover the all enveloping quality of Masaaki Kawashima's *Fundamentals of Men's Fashion Design*.

Much in life is a matter of timing, and an ironic phenomenon has happened with the publication of this book. By waiting out the violent periods of change before publication, the book becomes an important tool to create designs effectively for all fashion markets.

The surge of consumerism and the social, creative and economic value of home sewing makes this reference work a treasure for everyone seriously interested in pursuing that craft.

There is not a student anywhere who will not benefit by the clarity of this reference book. To design clothes intelligently one must have mastered the tools and techniques of the art.

Masaaki Kawashima has, in *Fundamentals of Men's Fashion Design*, created a guide to tailored clothes that has long been needed.

Robert L. Green

ACKNOWLEDGEMENTS

No book issues from one hand or from one individual's experiences. Accordingly, I am indebted to the following friends and colleagues for the help, suggestions, inspiration and patience which they have offered me so generously during the preparation of this book: Ernestine Kopp, Edmund Roberts, Hilda Friedman, Pauline Newman, Shirley Goodman, Muriel Golden, Nancy Margolis, Kenichi Aoki, Randy Dana, Itsuko Aoki, and Shelly Ruchlin and Ed Gold of Fairchild Publications. I am, of course, especially grateful to Robert L. Green for his kind Foreword.

INTRODUCTION

This book presents to the classroom teacher and student, and also to those in the fashion industry and at home who may use it, a simplified method of pattern making for men's clothes and a guide to the fundamentals of men's fashions. The aim of the book is to begin at the very beginning and lead the person who works with it from the most elementary parts of men's fashion to the point where he or she may be able to create designs on paper and then translate these designs into an ensemble of men's wear. Because of the great variety in human shapes and proportions, the author has worked from "average" or "standard" or "normal" sizes. The author understands that these exist only in theory and hopes that the reader will adjust what is here presented to his or her own needs. The following paragraphs discuss the organization of the book and how the reader should use it.

The Organization and Use of the Book

For the convenience of the reader, the material presented is divided into seven sections (as may be noted from a glance at the detailed Table of Contents). Each section concentrates upon the fundamentals of a basic step or element in the process of creating men's clothes. Each element is described by means of a text, diagrams, and drawings. In most cases, the reader will note that the design drawing and text are on the left-hand page (the even-numbered pages), while the technical diagrams, with a step-by-step description, are on the right-hand page (on the odd-numbered pages). A brief description of each section follows.

Section I: Drafting Equipment and Body Measurements

Before learning the skills of a professional, one must have at hand the basic tools of the trade. This section lists the tools necessary for the beginner, shows how to use these tools to take accurate body measurements and draft them correctly on paper, and presents a size chart based on standards widely used in the fashion industry. The size chart may be used for the design of jackets, pants, shirts, sleeves, suits, and coats.

Section II: Pattern Fundamentals

Before the beginning student starts to make a basic pattern or "sloper," he or she will need at least to know the uses of the fourteen pattern fundamentals illustrated in this section. Thus, Section II is a stepping-stone from Section I, the basic tools of the trade, to Section III, which starts with the basic design or sloper for pants.

Section III: Fundamentals of Pants Design

After the student has learned the basic details from which a design can be made, then he or she is ready for the next step—the pants sloper, the point at which the designer starts to make clothes for men. One begins with the pants sloper because it is relatively the easiest of the three basic slopers (pants, jacket, and sleeve). Attention is given to such details as pockets and cuffs and their variations and the back-view design for pants.

Section IV: Fundamentals of Jacket Design

Of the three basic slopers, the jacket design is the most complicated because it has more details and lines in its composition than the other two. Five basic jacket designs are presented in this section: 1) casual or sack, 2) basic, 3) fitted, 4) torso-cut, and 5) cape. Variations in design and composition details, such as buttonholes and pockets, are described and illustrated.

Section V: Fundamentals of Sleeve Design

The sleeve sloper stands between the pants and jacket slopers because it is not as simple as the former nor as complicated as the latter. Here, four basic sleeve slopers are dealt with: 1) the one-piece, 2) the two-piece, 3) the three-piece, and 4) the raglan. Just as with the pants and jacket slopers, the basic details of the sleeve sloper are described by words and diagrams.

Section VI: Fundamentals of Collar and Neckline Design

Before beginning the study of this section, the reader should be thoroughly acquainted with Section IV: The Fundamentals of Jacket Design. The collar and neckline design were purposely kept separate in order that the student could first master the skills of assembling a jacket. Some fourteen basic collar and neckline designs and their variations are illustrated, along with their different measurements

Section VII: Fundamentals of Jacket Back-View Design

Because of the extensive variety of back-view designs for the jacket, this section was added in addition to the section on the jacket. Vents, pleats, belts, and yokes, along with their variations are shown here.

TABLE OF CONTENTS

Page

METRIC CONVERSION TABLE (Inches to Centimeters)   x

SECTION I   **DRAFTING EQUIPMENT AND BODY MEASUREMENT**
Drafting Tools 1
Measurements 4
Men's Suit Measurements (Regular)...................................... 6
Men's Suit Measurements (Short).. 8
Men's Suit Measurements (Long) 10

SECTION II   **PATTERN FUNDAMENTALS**
Jacket Parts 12
Pants and Sleeve Parts 13
Jacket Grain Line 14
Sleeve and Pants Grain Line 15
Jacket and Sleeve Cross Marks 16
Pants Cross Mark 17
Jacket Seam Allowance 18
Torso Jacket Seam Allowance... 19
Sleeve Seam Allowance 20
Pants Seam Allowance 21
Tailored Jacket Facing 22
Casual Jacket Facing 23
Blending Procedure... 24
Squaring-off Procedure 25

SECTION III   **FUNDAMENTALS OF PANTS DESIGN**
Basic Pants Sloper 26
Pants Waist Dart 30
Pleated Pants 32
Double Pleated Pants 34
Basic Pants 36
Cuffed Basic Pants with Patch Pocket 38
Basic Pants with Diagonal Pocket.. 40
Basic Straight Pants 42
Straight Pants with Double Piping Pocket 44
Cuffed Straight Pants with Vertical Piping Pocket 46
Straight Pants Variation with Welt Pocket 48
Flare Pants 50
Pleated Flare Pants (A).. 52
Pleated Flare Pants (B).. 54
Casual Shorts 56
Walking Shorts 58
Short Knickers 60
Long Knickers 62

SECTION IV   **FUNDAMENTALS OF JACKET DESIGN**

Basic Jacket Sloper... 64
Jacket Sloper 68
High and Low Armholes.. 70
Shifting Shoulder Line 71
Cardigan Jacket 72
Workmen's Jacket 74
Buttoned Cardigan Jacket with Patch Pocket 76
Collared Cardigan Jacket 78
Tennis Jacket 80
Casual Jacket Drafting Procedure 82
Single Breasted Blazer 84
Double Breasted Blazer 86
One Button Single Breasted Italian Cut Jacket 88
Two Button Continental Jacket 90
Three Button Single Breasted Italian Cut Jacket 92
Two Button Double Breasted Continental Jacket 94
Double Breasted Continental Jacket 96
Italian Cut Jacket 98
Draped Double Breasted Jacket 100
Ivy League Jacket 102
Basic Jacket Drafting Procedure..................................... 104
Fitted Jacket Drafting Procedure 105
Shoulder Torso Cut Jacket.. 106
Neckline Torso Cut Jacket 108
Center Front Torso Cut Jacket 110
Armhole Torso Cut Jacket 112
Armhole Torso Cut Jacket Variation 114
Four Basic Torso Cut Jackets... 116
Dinner Jacket.. 118
Link Front Evening Jacket... 120
Basic Cape 122
Long Flared Cape 124
Tailored Cape.. 126
Buttonhole Design for Casual Jacket 128
Buttonhole Design for Tailored Jacket 130
Pockets 132

SECTION V   **FUNDAMENTALS OF SLEEVE DESIGN**

Basic Sleeve Sloper... 136
One Piece Sleeve 140
Cuffed Sleeve 142
Two Piece Sleeve.. 144
Semi Raglan Sleeve 148
Basic Raglan Sleeve 150
Raglan Sleeve Variation 158
One-Piece Raglan Sleeve.. 160
Cuff Designs... 162

SECTION VI   **FUNDAMENTALS OF NECKLINE AND COLLAR DESIGN**
Round Neckline 164
Square Neckline 165
V-Neckline 166
Boat Neckline 167
Basic Banded Collar Variation.. 168
Banded Collar Variation 170
Mandarin Collar Variation 172
Funnel Collar Variation 174
Convertible Collar Variation 176
Open Neck Convertible Collar Variation......................... 178
Continental Collar Variation 180
Shirt Collar Variation 182
Dress Shirt Collar Variation 184
Collar Parts and Notch Collar Size Variation 186
Notch Collar 188
Notch Collar Design 194

SECTION VII   **FUNDAMENTALS OF JACKET BACK-VIEW DESIGN**
Center Vents 200
Side Vents... 201
Jacket Back View, Set-in Belt with Darts Variation A and B. 202
Jacket Back View, Set-in Belt with Pleat Variation.............. 204
Jacket Back View, Yoke Variation A, B, C, and D 206

SECTION VIII   **FUNDAMENTALS OF VEST DESIGN**
Basic Vest 214
Formal Vest with Shawl Collar 216

ABOUT THE AUTHOR 218

METRIC CONVERSION TABLE (Inches to Centimeters)

Inches		1/16	1/8	1/4	3/8	1/2	5/8	3/4	7/8
		0.16	0.32	0.64	0.95	1.27	1.59	1.91	2.22
1	2.54	2.70	2.86	3.18	3.49	3.81	4.13	4.45	4.76
2	5.08	5.24	5.40	5.72	6.03	6.35	6.67	6.99	7.30
3	7.62	7.78	7.94	8.26	8.57	8.89	9.21	9.53	9.84
4	10.16	10.32	10.48	10.80	11.11	11.43	11.75	12.07	12.38
5	12.70	12.86	13.02	13.34	13.65	13.97	14.29	14.61	14.92
6	15.24	15.40	15.56	15.88	16.19	16.51	16.83	17.15	17.46
7	17.78	17.94	18.10	18.42	18.73	19.05	19.37	19.69	20.00
8	20.32	20.48	20.64	20.96	21.27	21.59	21.91	22.23	22.54
9	22.86	23.02	23.18	23.50	23.81	24.13	24.45	24.77	25.08
10	25.40	25.56	25.72	26.04	26.35	26.67	26.99	27.31	27.62
11	27.94	28.10	28.26	28.58	28.89	29.21	29.53	29.85	30.16
12	30.48	30.64	30.80	31.12	31.43	31.75	32.02	32.39	32.70
13	33.02	33.18	33.34	33.66	33.97	34.29	34.61	34.93	35.24
14	35.56	35.72	35.88	36.20	36.51	36.83	37.15	37.47	37.78
15	38.10	38.26	38.42	38.74	39.05	39.37	36.69	40.01	40.32
16	40.64	40.80	40.96	41.28	41.59	41.91	42.23	42.55	42.86
17	43.18	43.34	43.50	43.82	44.13	44.45	44.77	45.09	45.40
18	45.72	45.88	46.04	46.36	46.67	46.99	47.31	47.63	47.94
19	48.26	48.42	48.58	48.90	49.21	49.53	49.85	50.17	50.48
20	50.80	50.96	51.12	51.44	51.75	52.07	52.39	52.71	53.02
21	53.34	53.50	53.66	53.98	54.29	54.61	54.93	55.25	55.56
22	55.88	56.04	56.20	56.52	56.83	57.15	57.47	57.79	58.10
23	58.42	58.58	58.74	59.06	59.37	59.69	60.01	60.33	60.64
24	60.96	61.12	61.28	61.60	61.91	62.23	62.55	62.87	63.18
25	63.50	63.66	63.82	64.14	64.45	64.77	65.09	65.41	65.72
26	66.04	66.20	66.36	66.68	66.99	67.31	67.63	67.95	68.26
27	68.58	68.74	68.90	69.22	69.53	69.85	70.17	70.49	70.80
28	71.12	71.28	71.44	71.76	72.07	72.39	72.71	73.03	73.34
29	73.66	73.82	73.98	74.30	74.61	74.93	75.25	75.57	75.88
30	76.20	76.36	76.52	76.84	77.15	77.47	77.79	78.11	78.42
31	78.74	78.90	79.06	79.38	79.69	80.01	80.33	80.65	80.96
32	81.28	81.44	81.60	81.92	82.23	82.55	82.87	83.19	83.50
33	83.82	83.98	84.14	84.46	84.77	85.09	85.41	85.73	86.04
34	86.36	86.52	86.68	87.00	87.31	87.63	87.95	88.27	88.58
35	88.90	89.06	89.22	89.54	89.85	90.17	90.49	90.81	91.12
36	91.44	91.60	91.76	92.08	92.39	92.71	93.03	93.35	93.66
37	93.98	94.14	94.30	94.62	94.93	95.25	95.57	95.89	96.20
38	96.52	96.68	96.84	97.16	97.47	97.79	98.11	98.43	98.74
39	99.06	99.22	99.38	99.70	100.01	100.33	100.65	100.97	101.28
40	101.60	101.76	101.92	102.24	102.55	102.87	103.19	103.51	103.82
41	104.14	104.30	104.46	104.78	105.09	105.41	105.73	106.05	106.36
42	106.68	106.84	107.00	107.32	107.63	107.95	108.27	108.59	108.90
43	109.22	109.38	109.54	109.86	110.17	110.49	110.81	111.13	111.44
44	111.76	111.92	112.08	112.40	112.71	113.03	113.35	113.67	113.98
45	114.30	114.46	114.62	114.94	115.25	115.57	115.89	116.21	116.52
46	116.84	117.00	117.16	117.48	117.79	118.11	118.43	118.75	119.06
47	119.38	119.54	119.70	120.02	120.33	120.65	120.97	121.29	121.60
48	121.92	122.08	122.24	122.56	122.87	123.19	123.51	123.83	124.14
49	124.46	124.62	124.78	125.10	125.41	125.73	126.05	126.37	126.68
50	127.00	127.16	127.32	127.64	127.95	128.27	128.59	128.91	129.22
51	129.54	129.70	129.86	130.18	130.49	130.81	131.13	131.45	131.76
52	132.08	132.24	132.40	132.72	133.03	133.35	133.67	133.99	134.30
53	134.62	134.78	134.94	135.26	135.57	135.89	136.21	136.53	136.84
54	137.16	137.32	137.48	137.80	138.11	138.43	138.75	139.07	139.38
55	139.70	139.86	140.02	140.34	140.65	140.97	141.29	141.61	141.92
56	142.24	142.40	142.56	142.88	143.19	143.51	143.83	144.15	144.46
57	144.78	144.94	145.10	145.42	145.73	146.05	146.37	146.69	147.00
58	147.32	147.48	147.64	147.96	148.27	148.59	148.91	149.23	149.54
59	149.86	150.02	150.18	150.50	150.81	151.13	151.45	151.77	152.08
60	152.40	152.56	152.72	153.04	153.35	153.67	153.99	154.31	154.62

DRAFTING TOOLS

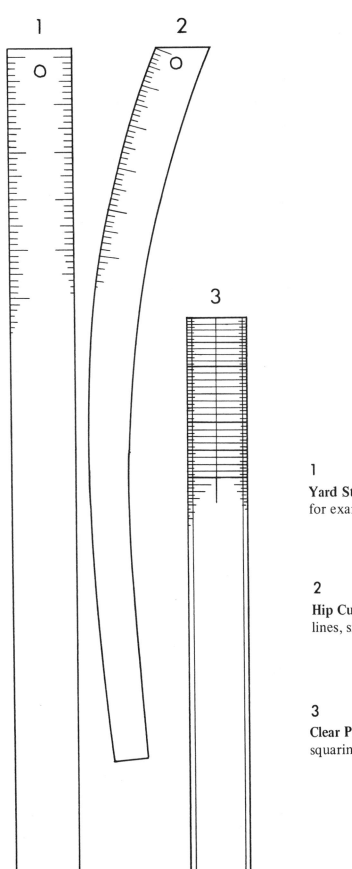

1

Yard Stick—Used to measure longer lengths; for example: pants and coats.

2

Hip Curve Ruler—Shallow curve for shoulders, hemlines, side seams, sleeves, and darts.

3

Clear Plastic Ruler—For visibility of measurements, squaring off and determining seam allowances.

DRAFTING TOOLS

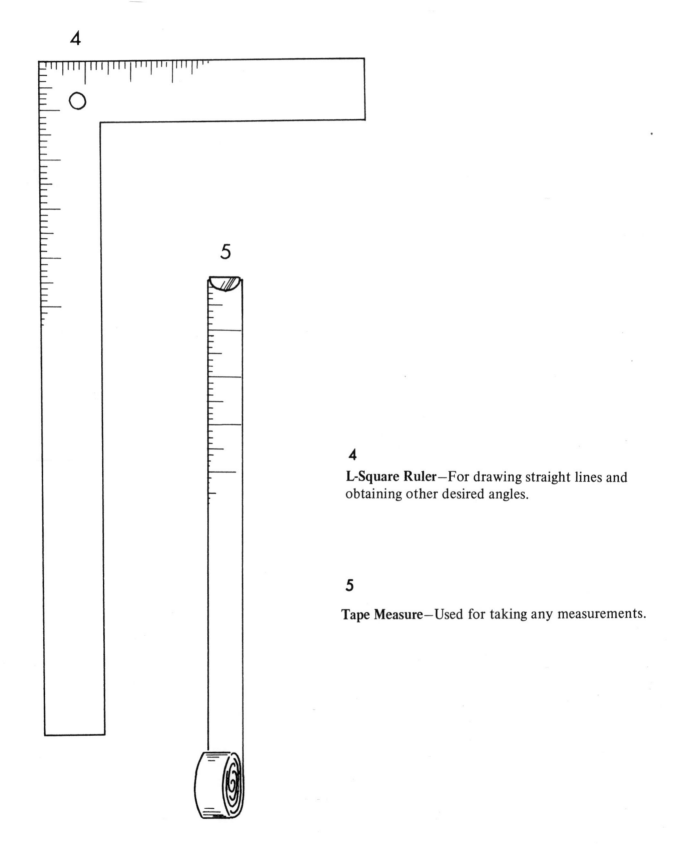

4

L-Square Ruler—For drawing straight lines and obtaining other desired angles.

5

Tape Measure—Used for taking any measurements.

DRAFTING TOOLS

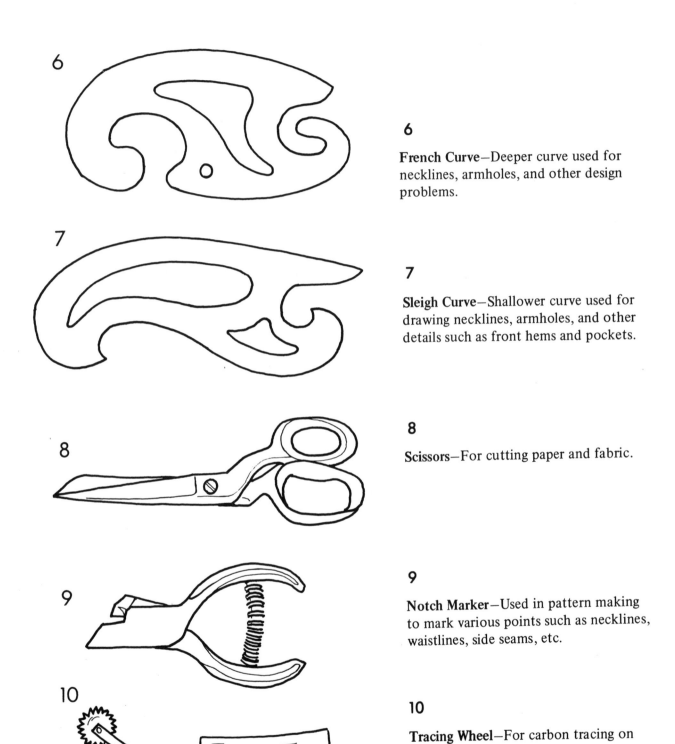

6

French Curve—Deeper curve used for necklines, armholes, and other design problems.

7

Sleigh Curve—Shallower curve used for drawing necklines, armholes, and other details such as front hems and pockets.

8

Scissors—For cutting paper and fabric.

9

Notch Marker—Used in pattern making to mark various points such as necklines, waistlines, side seams, etc.

10

Tracing Wheel—For carbon tracing on muslin and paper patterns.

MEASUREMENTS

Jacket

A = Chest circumference

B = Waist circumference

C = Front chest measurement armhole to armhole

D = Sleeve length

E = Jacket length

F = Back waist length

G = Shoulder blade armhole to armhole

H = Shoulder length neck to armhole

Pants

I = Crotch depth. Take measurement by sitting person on solid-
based flat chair surface. Measure from waist to chair surface.

J = Full pant length waist to hem

K = Hip measurement is usually 8" below waist

MEASUREMENTS

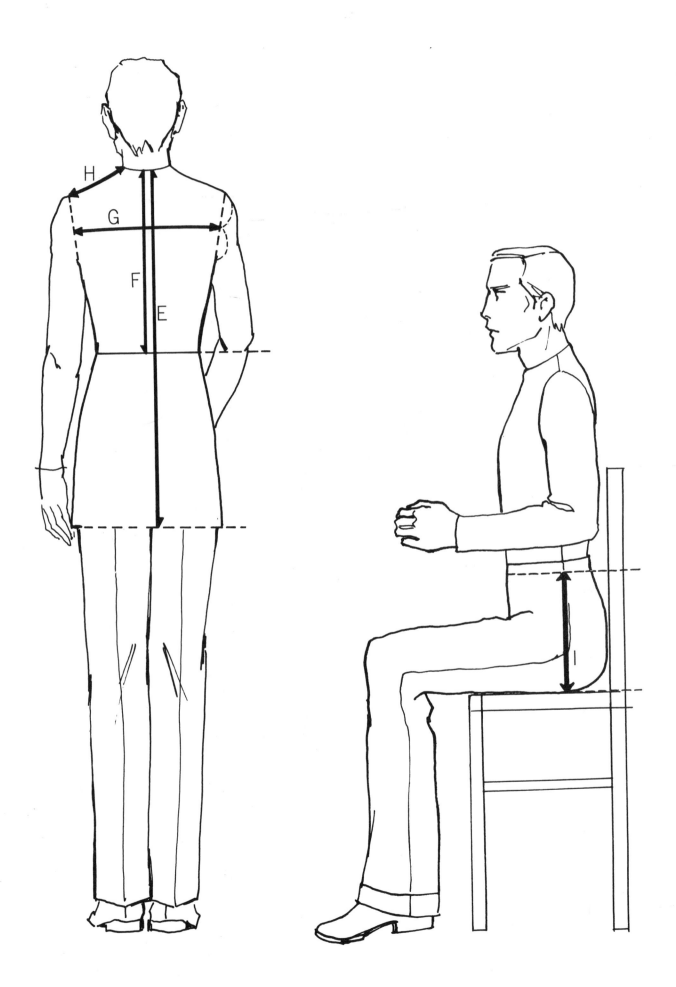

6

MEN'S SUIT AND COAT MEASUREMENTS
REGULAR

SIZE	34	36	38	40	42	44
CHEST CIRCUMFERENCE	34	36	38	40	42	44
WAIST	28	30	32	34	36	38
HIP	34	36	38	40	42	44
FRONT CHEST	$14\frac{1}{2}$	15	$15\frac{1}{2}$	16	$16\frac{1}{2}$	17
BACK WAIST LENGTH	$17\frac{1}{2}$	$17\frac{3}{4}$	18	$18\frac{1}{4}$	$18\frac{1}{2}$	$18\frac{3}{4}$
SHOULDER BLADE	16	$16\frac{1}{2}$	17	$17\frac{1}{2}$	18	$18\frac{1}{2}$
SHOULDER LENGTH	$5\frac{7}{8}$	6	$6\frac{1}{8}$	$6\frac{1}{4}$	$6\frac{3}{8}$	$6\frac{1}{2}$
JACKET LENGTH	$29\frac{3}{4}$	30	$30\frac{1}{4}$	$30\frac{1}{2}$	$30\frac{3}{4}$	31
COAT LENGTH	ACCORDING TO DESIGN					
JACKET SLEEVE FULL LENGTH	$23\frac{3}{8}$	$23\frac{5}{8}$	$23\frac{7}{8}$	$24\frac{1}{8}$	$24\frac{3}{8}$	$24\frac{5}{8}$
COAT SLEEVE FULL LENGTH	JACKET SLEEVE LENGTH PLUS 3/8 INCH					
CROTCH DEPTH	$9\frac{3}{4}$	10	$10\frac{1}{4}$	$10\frac{1}{2}$	$10\frac{3}{4}$	11
PANTS FULL LENGTH	$41\frac{1}{2}$	42	$42\frac{1}{2}$	43	$43\frac{1}{2}$	44

MEN'S SUIT AND COAT MEASUREMENTS
REGULAR

SIZE	35	37	39	41	43	45
CHEST CIRCUMFERENCE	35	37	39	41	43	45
WAIST	29	31	33	35	37	39
HIP	35	37	39	41	43	45
FRONT CHEST	$14\frac{3}{4}$	$15\frac{1}{4}$	$15\frac{3}{4}$	$16\frac{1}{4}$	$16\frac{3}{4}$	$17\frac{1}{4}$
BACK WAIST LENGTH	$17\frac{5}{8}$	$17\frac{7}{8}$	$18\frac{1}{8}$	$18\frac{3}{8}$	$18\frac{5}{8}$	$18\frac{7}{8}$
SHOULDER BLADE	$16\frac{1}{4}$	$16\frac{3}{4}$	$17\frac{1}{4}$	$17\frac{3}{4}$	$18\frac{1}{4}$	$18\frac{3}{4}$
SHOULDER LENGTH	$5\frac{15}{16}$	$6\frac{1}{16}$	$6\frac{3}{16}$	$6\frac{5}{16}$	$6\frac{7}{16}$	$6\frac{9}{16}$
JACKET LENGTH	$29\frac{7}{8}$	$30\frac{1}{8}$	$30\frac{3}{8}$	$30\frac{5}{8}$	$30\frac{7}{8}$	$31\frac{1}{8}$
COAT LENGTH	ACCORDING TO DESIGN					
JACKET SLEEVE FULL LENGTH	$23\frac{1}{2}$	$23\frac{3}{4}$	24	$24\frac{1}{4}$	$24\frac{1}{2}$	$24\frac{3}{4}$
COAT SLEEVE FULL LENGTH	JACKET SLEEVE LENGTH PLUS 3/8 INCH					
CROTCH DEPTH	$9\frac{7}{8}$	$10\frac{1}{8}$	$10\frac{3}{8}$	$10\frac{5}{8}$	$10\frac{7}{8}$	$11\frac{1}{8}$
PANTS FULL LENGTH	$41\frac{3}{4}$	$42\frac{1}{4}$	$42\frac{3}{4}$	$43\frac{1}{4}$	$43\frac{3}{4}$	$44\frac{1}{4}$

8

MEN'S SUIT AND COAT MEASUREMENTS
SHORT

SIZE	34	36	38	40	42	44
CHEST CIRCUMFERENCE	34	36	38	40	42	44
WAIST	28	30	32	34	36	38
HIP	34	36	38	40	42	44
FRONT CHEST	$14\frac{1}{2}$	15	$15\frac{1}{2}$	16	$16\frac{1}{2}$	17
BACK WAIST LENGTH	$16\frac{1}{2}$	$16\frac{3}{4}$	17	$17\frac{1}{4}$	$17\frac{1}{2}$	$17\frac{3}{4}$
SHOULDER BLADE	16	$16\frac{1}{2}$	17	$17\frac{1}{2}$	18	$18\frac{1}{2}$
SHOULDER LENGTH	$5\frac{7}{8}$	6	$6\frac{1}{8}$	$6\frac{1}{4}$	$6\frac{3}{8}$	$6\frac{1}{2}$
JACKET LENGTH	$28\frac{3}{4}$	29	$29\frac{1}{4}$	$29\frac{1}{2}$	$29\frac{3}{4}$	30
COAT LENGTH	ACCORDING TO DESIGN					
JACKET SLEEVE FULL LENGTH	$22\frac{3}{8}$	$22\frac{5}{8}$	$22\frac{7}{8}$	$23\frac{1}{8}$	$23\frac{3}{8}$	$23\frac{5}{8}$
COAT SLEEVE FULL LENGTH	JACKET SLEEVE LENGTH PLUS 3/8 INCH					
CROTCH DEPTH	$9\frac{1}{4}$	$9\frac{1}{2}$	$9\frac{3}{4}$	10	$10\frac{1}{4}$	$10\frac{1}{2}$
PANTS FULL LENGTH	41	$41\frac{1}{2}$	42	$42\frac{1}{2}$	43	$43\frac{1}{2}$

MEN'S SUIT AND COAT MEASUREMENTS
SHORT

SIZE	35	37	39	41	43	45
CHEST CIRCUMFERENCE	35	37	39	41	43	45
WAIST	29	31	33	35	37	39
HIP	35	37	39	41	43	45
FRONT CHEST	$14\frac{3}{4}$	$15\frac{1}{4}$	$15\frac{3}{4}$	$16\frac{1}{4}$	$16\frac{3}{4}$	$17\frac{1}{4}$
BACK WAIST LENGTH	$16\frac{5}{8}$	$16\frac{7}{8}$	$17\frac{1}{8}$	$17\frac{3}{8}$	$17\frac{5}{8}$	$17\frac{7}{8}$
SHOULDER BLADE	$16\frac{1}{4}$	$16\frac{3}{4}$	$17\frac{1}{4}$	$17\frac{3}{4}$	$18\frac{1}{4}$	$18\frac{3}{4}$
SHOULDER LENGTH	$5\frac{15}{16}$	$6\frac{1}{16}$	$6\frac{3}{16}$	$6\frac{5}{16}$	$6\frac{7}{16}$	$6\frac{9}{16}$
JACKET LENGTH	$28\frac{7}{8}$	$29\frac{1}{8}$	$29\frac{3}{8}$	$29\frac{5}{8}$	$29\frac{7}{8}$	$30\frac{9}{8}$
COAT LENGTH	ACCORDING TO DESIGN					
JACKET SLEEVE FULL LENGTH	$22\frac{1}{2}$	$22\frac{3}{4}$	23	$23\frac{1}{4}$	$23\frac{1}{2}$	$23\frac{3}{4}$
COAT SLEEVE FULL LENGTH	JACKET SLEEVE LENGTH PLUS 3/8 INCH					
CROTCH DEPTH	$9\frac{3}{8}$	$9\frac{5}{8}$	$9\frac{7}{8}$	$10\frac{1}{8}$	$10\frac{3}{8}$	$10\frac{5}{8}$
PANTS FULL LENGTH	$41\frac{1}{4}$	$41\frac{3}{4}$	$42\frac{1}{4}$	$42\frac{3}{4}$	$43\frac{1}{4}$	$43\frac{3}{4}$

MEN'S SUIT AND COAT MEASUREMENTS
LONG

SIZE	34	36	38	40	42	44
CHEST CIRCUMFERENCE	34	36	38	40	42	44
WAIST	28	30	32	34	36	38
HIP	34	36	38	40	42	44
FRONT CHEST	$14\frac{1}{2}$	15	$15\frac{1}{2}$	16	$16\frac{1}{2}$	17
BACK WAIST LENGTH	$18\frac{1}{2}$	$18\frac{3}{4}$	19	$19\frac{1}{4}$	$19\frac{1}{2}$	$19\frac{3}{4}$
SHOULDER BLADE	16	$16\frac{1}{2}$	17	$17\frac{1}{2}$	18	$18\frac{1}{2}$
SHOULDER LENGTH	$5\frac{7}{8}$	6	$6\frac{1}{8}$	$6\frac{1}{4}$	$6\frac{3}{8}$	$6\frac{1}{2}$
JACKET LENGTH	$30\frac{3}{4}$	31	$31\frac{1}{4}$	$31\frac{1}{2}$	$31\frac{3}{4}$	32
COAT LENGTH	ACCORDING TO DESIGN					
JACKET SLEEVE FULL LENGTH	$24\frac{3}{8}$	$24\frac{5}{8}$	$24\frac{7}{8}$	$25\frac{1}{8}$	$25\frac{3}{8}$	$25\frac{5}{8}$
COAT SLEEVE FULL LENGTH	JACKET SLEEVE LENGTH PLUS 3/8 INCH					
CROTCH DEPTH	$10\frac{1}{4}$	$10\frac{1}{2}$	$10\frac{3}{4}$	11	$11\frac{1}{4}$	$11\frac{1}{2}$
PANTS FULL LENGTH	42	$42\frac{1}{2}$	43	$43\frac{1}{2}$	44	$44\frac{1}{2}$

MEN'S SUIT AND COAT MEASUREMENTS
LONG

SIZE	35	37	39	41	43	45
CHEST CIRCUMFERENCE	35	37	39	41	43	45
WAIST	29	31	33	35	37	39
HIP	35	37	39	41	43	45
FRONT CHEST	$14\frac{3}{4}$	$15\frac{1}{4}$	$15\frac{3}{4}$	$16\frac{1}{4}$	$16\frac{3}{4}$	$17\frac{1}{4}$
BACK WAIST LENGTH	$18\frac{5}{8}$	$18\frac{7}{8}$	$19\frac{1}{8}$	$19\frac{3}{8}$	$19\frac{5}{8}$	$19\frac{7}{8}$
SHOULDER BLADE	16	$16\frac{1}{2}$	17	$17\frac{1}{2}$	18	$18\frac{1}{2}$
SHOULDER LENGTH	$5\frac{7}{8}$	6	$6\frac{1}{8}$	$6\frac{1}{4}$	$6\frac{3}{8}$	$6\frac{1}{2}$
JACKET LENGTH	$30\frac{3}{4}$	31	$31\frac{1}{4}$	$31\frac{1}{2}$	$31\frac{3}{4}$	32
COAT LENGTH	ACCORDING TO DESIGN					
JACKET SLEEVE FULL LENGTH	$24\frac{3}{8}$	$24\frac{5}{8}$	$24\frac{7}{8}$	$25\frac{1}{8}$	$25\frac{3}{8}$	$25\frac{5}{8}$
COAT SLEEVE FULL LENGTH	JACKET SLEEVE LENGTH PLUS 3/8 INCH					
CROTCH DEPTH	$10\frac{1}{4}$	$10\frac{1}{2}$	$10\frac{3}{4}$	11	$11\frac{1}{4}$	$11\frac{1}{2}$
PANTS FULL LENGTH	42	$42\frac{1}{2}$	43	$43\frac{1}{2}$	44	$44\frac{1}{2}$

JACKET PARTS

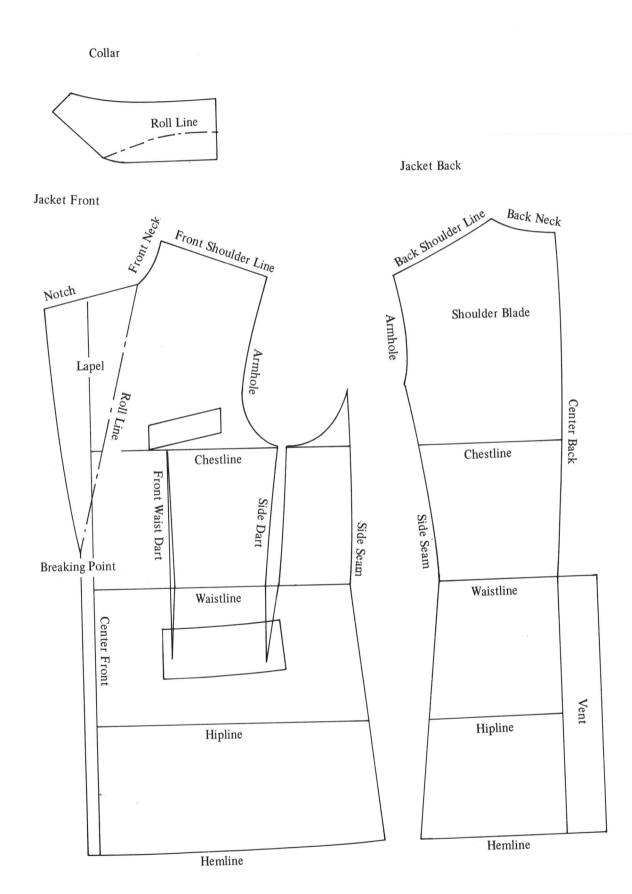

Collar

Roll Line

Jacket Back

Jacket Front

Front Neck

Front Shoulder Line

Back Shoulder Line

Back Neck

Notch

Shoulder Blade

Lapel

Armhole

Armhole

Roll Line

Chestline

Center Back

Chestline

Front Waist Dart

Side Dart

Side Seam

Side Seam

Breaking Point

Waistline

Waistline

Center Front

Vent

Hipline

Hipline

Hemline

Hemline

PANTS AND SLEEVE PARTS

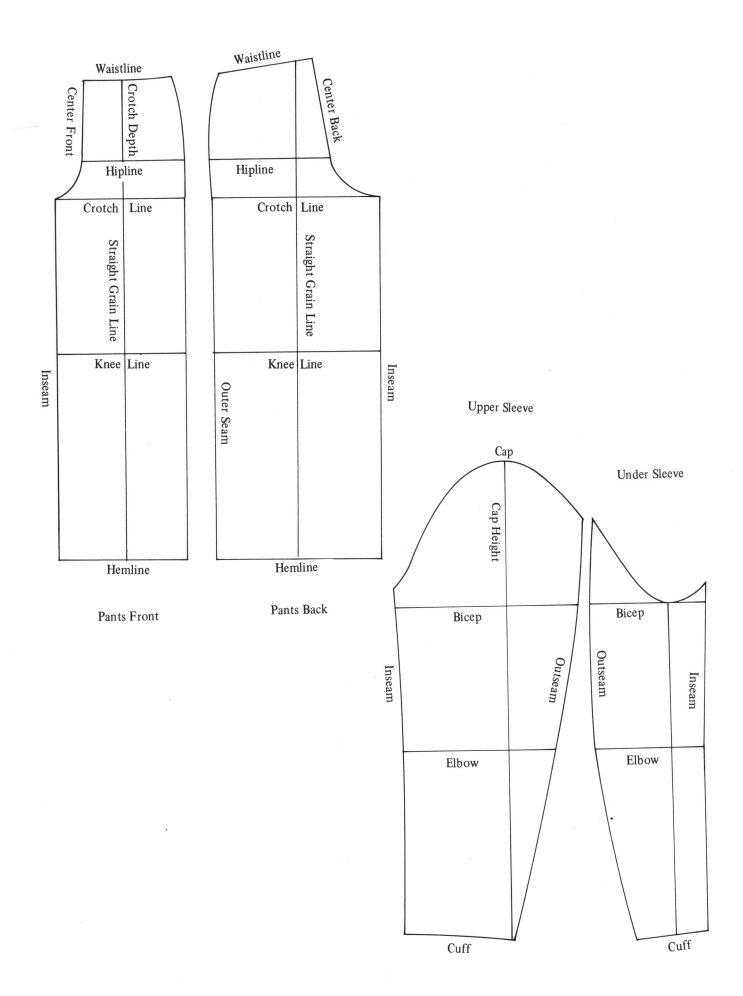

Pants Front

Pants Back

JACKET GRAIN LINE

Top Collar

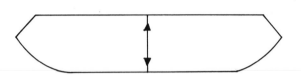

Under Collar

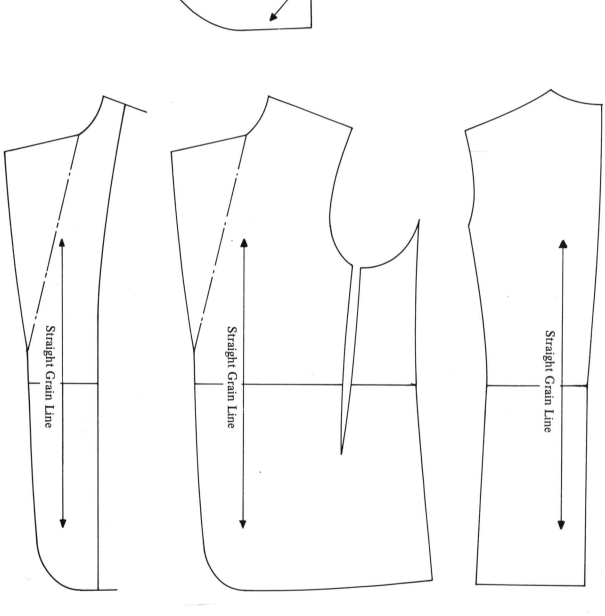

Facing   Jacket Front   Jacket Back

SLEEVE AND PANTS GRAIN LINE

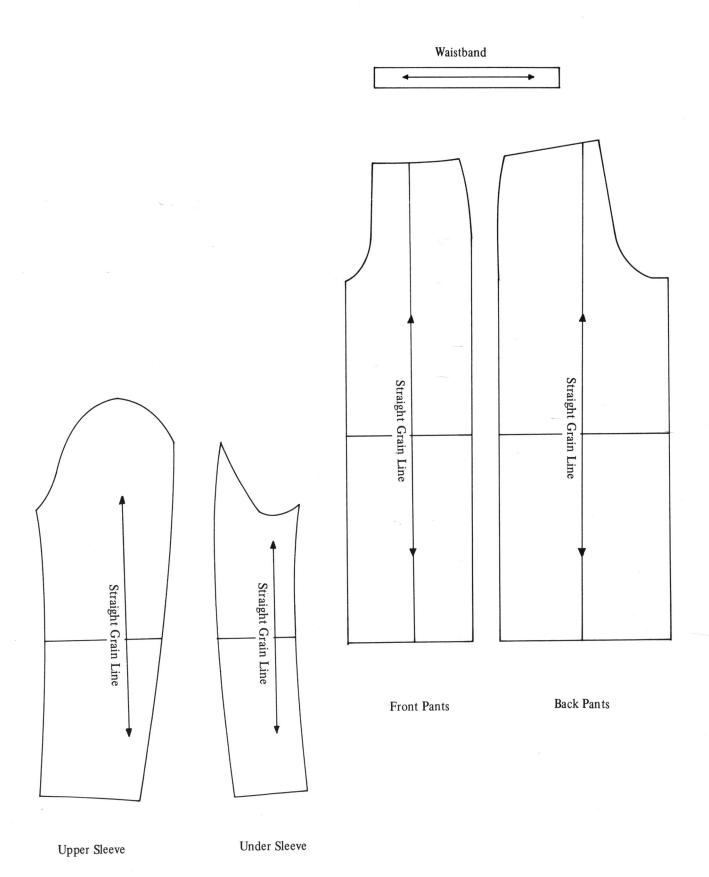

Waistband

Straight Grain Line

Straight Grain Line

Front Pants

Back Pants

Straight Grain Line

Straight Grain Line

Upper Sleeve

Under Sleeve

JACKET and SLEEVE CROSS MARKS

Collar

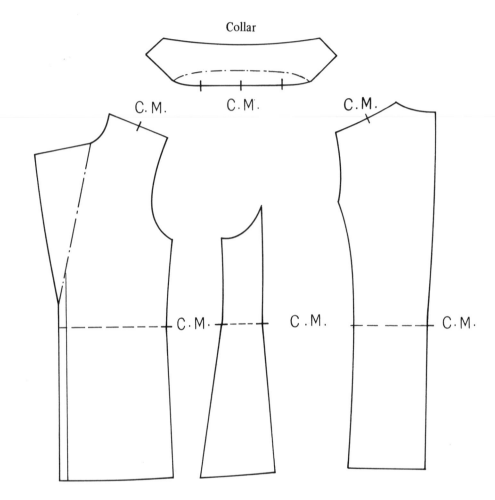

Front Jacket   Side Panel   Back Jacket

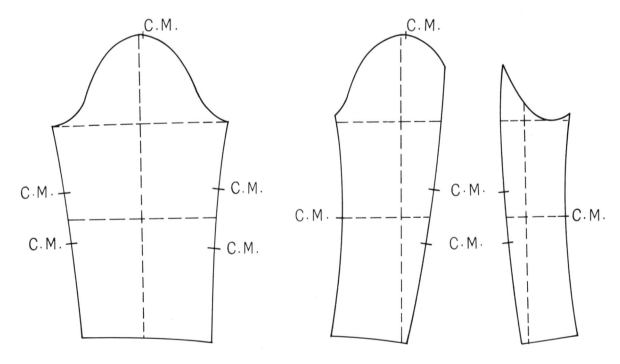

One-Piece Sleeve   Two-Piece Sleeve

PANTS CROSS MARKS

Waistband

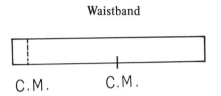

C.M.   C.M.

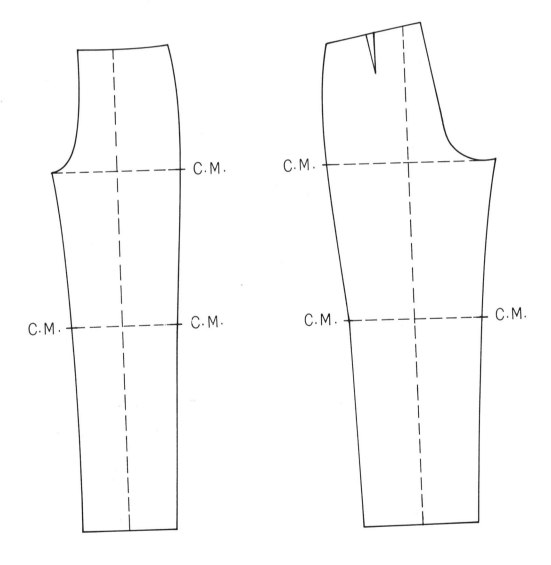

Front Pants   Back Pants

JACKET SEAM ALLOWANCE

Note: These seam allowances are for finished garments. For first fitting add extra seam allowances.

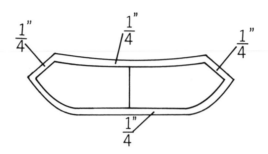

Top Collar

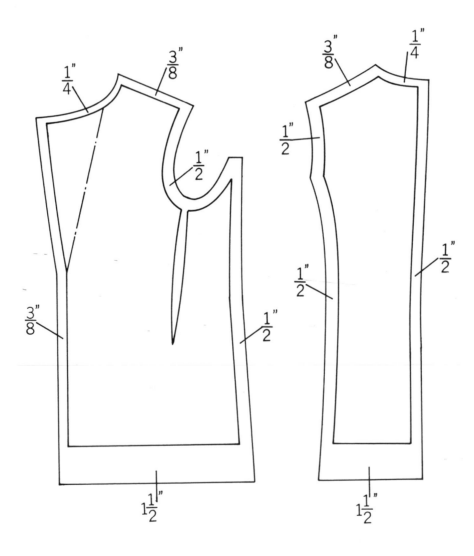

Jacket Front   Jacket Back

TORSO JACKET SEAM ALLOWANCE

Note: These seam allowances are for finished garments. For first fitting add extra seam allowances.

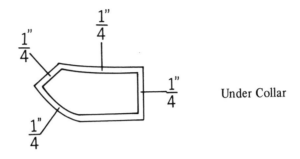

Under Collar

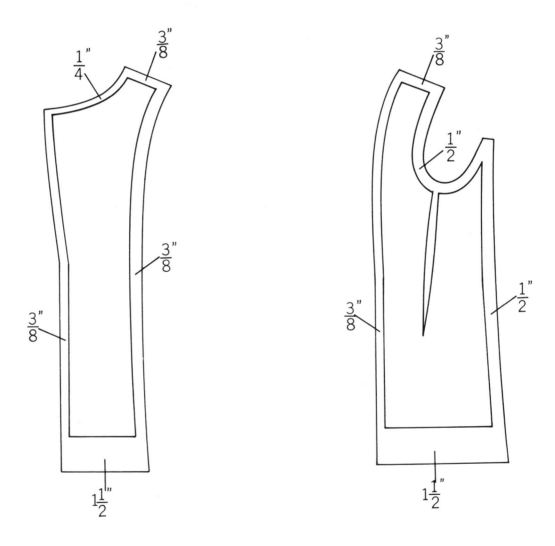

Jacket Front

Jacket Side Panel

SLEEVE SEAM ALLOWANCE

Note: These seam allowances are for finished garments. For first fitting add extra seam allowances.

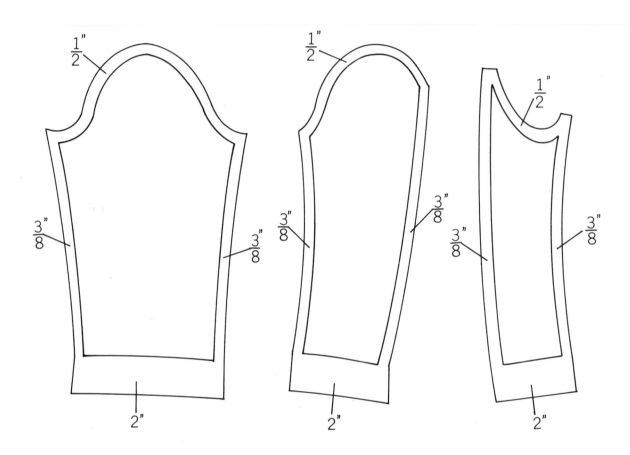

One-Piece Sleeve

Two-Piece Sleeve

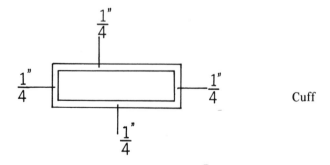

Cuff

PANTS SEAM ALLOWANCE

Note: These seam allowances are for finished garments. For first fitting add extra seam allowances.

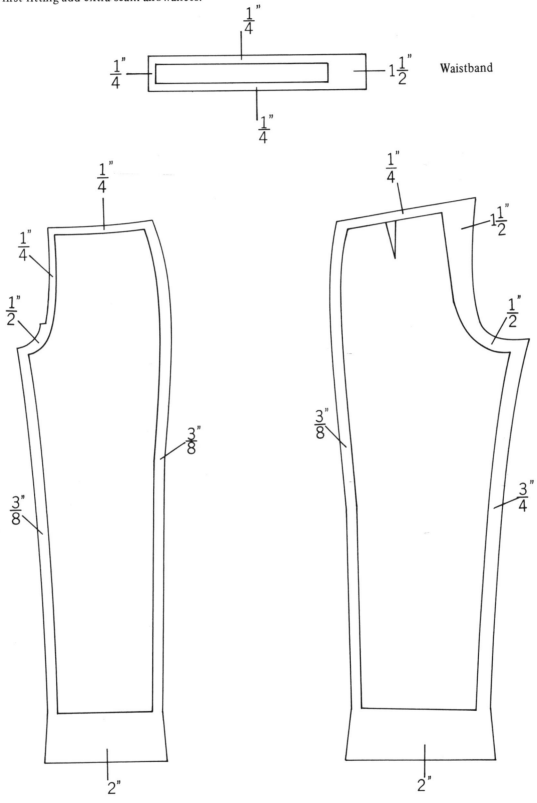

Waistband

Front Pants

Back Pants

22

TAILORED JACKET FACING

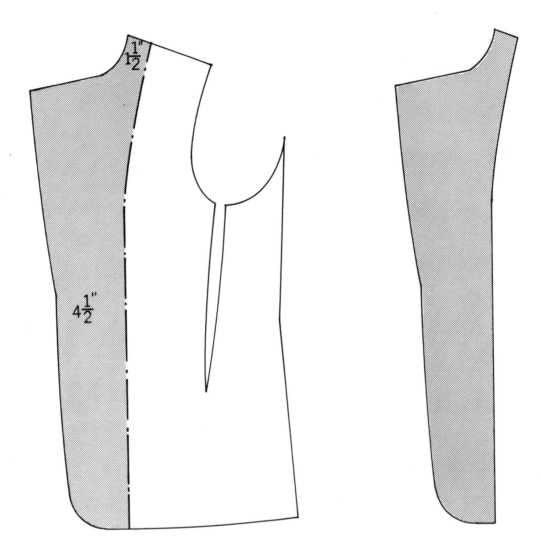

Jacket Front

Facing

CASUAL JACKET FACING

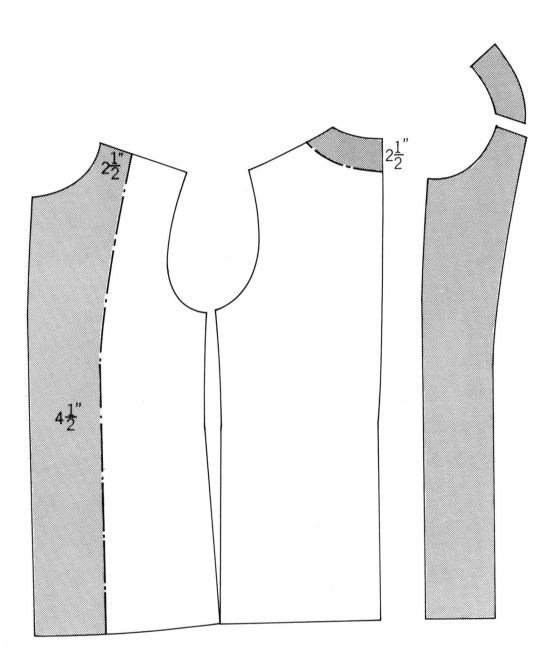

$2\frac{1}{2}$"

$2\frac{1}{2}$"

$4\frac{1}{2}$"

Jacket Front   Jacket Back   Facing

BLENDING PROCEDURE

DIAGRAM A   **DIAGRAM B**

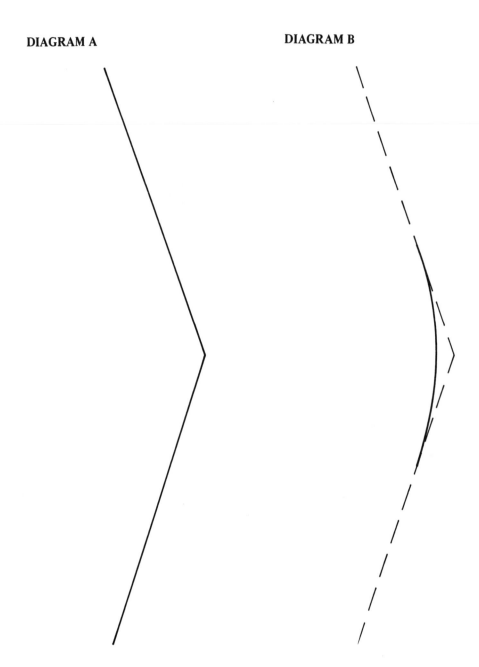

When lines intersect and create an angle, a smooth
"blended" line is needed. See **Diagram A**. This line
gives continuity to your patterns. See **Diagram B**.

All patterns in this book should blend connecting points
with a curve to form smooth, clean lines.

SQUARING-OFF PROCEDURE

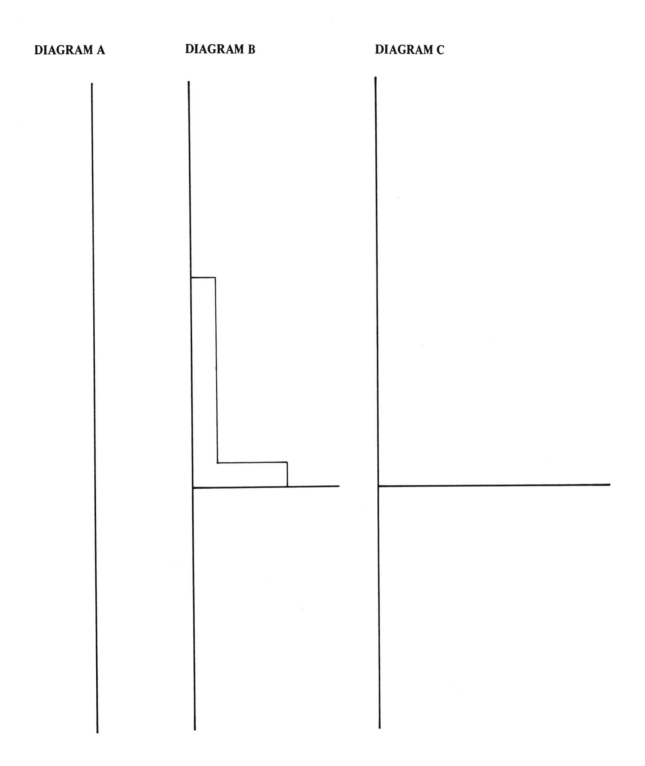

DIAGRAM A   **DIAGRAM B**   **DIAGRAM C**

Place L-square.
Draw a line on right angle.   Remove L-square.

BASIC PANTS SLOPER

In order to draft Basic Sloper, the following measurements are needed:

Waist.
Hip.
Crotch Depth.
Full Length (outer side seam, waist to hem).

See **Size Chart**, pages 6-7.

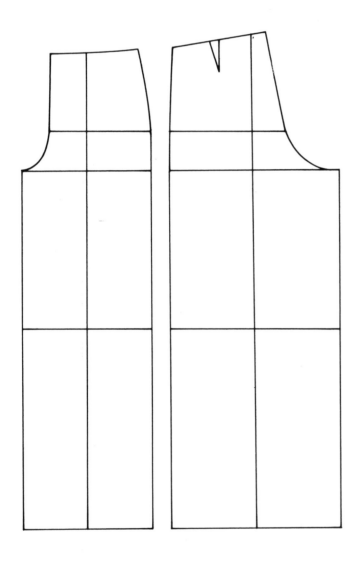

Front Pants   Back Pants

DIAGRAM A
Front
A = Waist.
D = Hip.
C = Crotch Depth.
F = Knee
B = Hem.
A to B = Full length.
A to C = Crotch depth.
C to D = 1/3 A to C.
E = 1/2 C to B.
F to E = 2".
Square off from A, D, C, F, and B towards left.
C to G = 1/4 hip.
G to H = 1/4 C to G.
I = 1/2 C to H.

DIAGRAM B
To locate K and J square up and down from I thus establishing straight grain and crease line.
Square up from G to L.
Connect O to H.
Connect G to P to form a 45° angle.
P to Q = 1/3 P to G.
Square H down to M.
H to M = inseam.
N = inseam on knee line.

DIAGRAM—Basic Pants Sloper

A

B

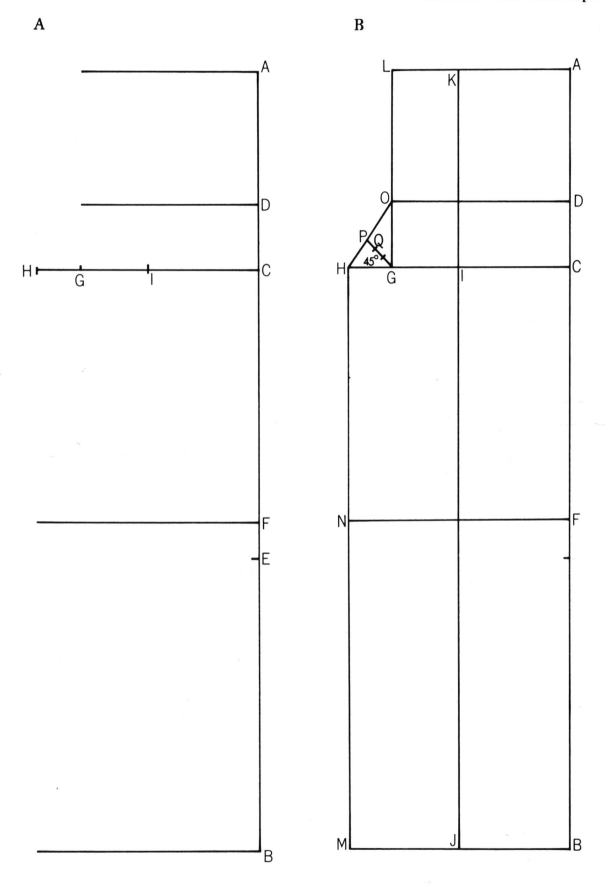

BASIC PANTS SLOPER

DIAGRAM C

L to R = 5/4".
Connect R to O with straight line.
Connect O to Q to H with sleigh curve to finish center front.
R to S = 1/4 waist.
S to T = 1/4".
Connect T to K with hip curve ruler to finish waistline.
Connect T to C with hip curve ruler to finish front pants.

DIAGRAM D

Back Pants

G = Starting point for back panel (center front at crotch depth line).
G to 1 = 3/8".
2 = 1/2 R to K.
Connect 1 to 2 with straight line and extend line upward for 4" to 5".
2 to 3 = 2 to R.
P to 4 = 1/2 P to G.
5 = hip line.
Connect 3 to 5 with straight line.
H to 6 = H to G -1/2".
Connect 5 to 4 and 4 to 6 with sleigh curve ruler.
C to 7 = H to 6.
3 to 8 = 1/4 waist + 3/4" for a dart.
8 = extended point 1/4" above original waist, at same height as T.
Connect 3 to 8 with straight line.
Connect 8 to 7 with shallow part of hip curve ruler.
3 to 9 = 1/2 3 to 8.
9 to 10 = 3/4" toward 8.
9 to 11 = 1/2 9 to 10.
Square off from 11 to 12 for 3".
Connect 9 to 12.
Connect 10 to 12 to finish darts.
13 to 14 = 6 to 7.
Connect 6 to 13.
Connect 7 to 14.

Waist Band

A to B = front waist measurement.
B = side seam.
B to C = back waist measurement.
A to D = width of band according to your design.

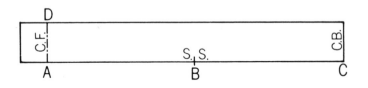

DIAGRAM—Basic Pants Sloper

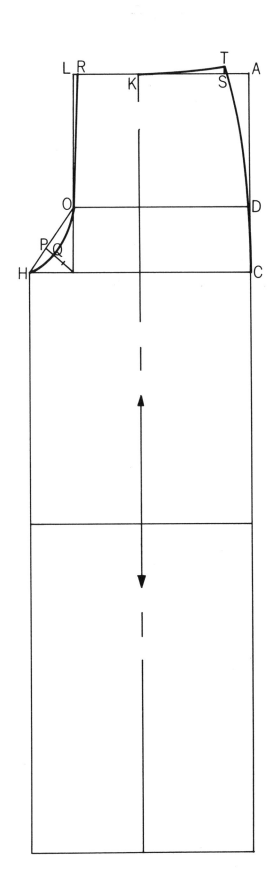

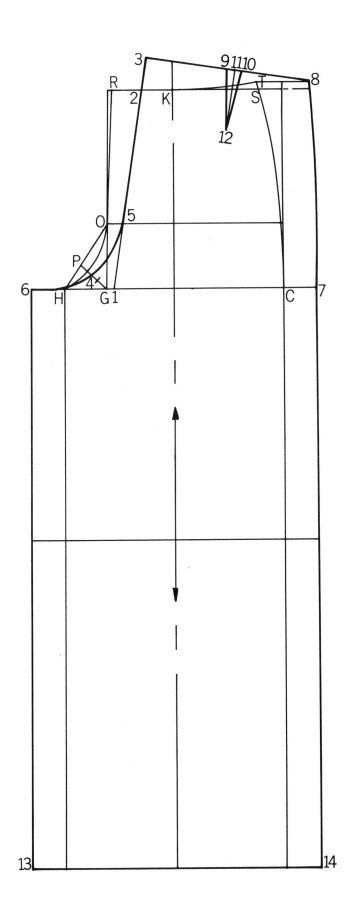

PANTS WAIST DART

Outline front pants sloper.

DIAGRAM A

A = center of dart and grainline at waist.
A to B = 3/8".
A to C = 3/8".
A to D = 3" for dart length.
E to F = 3/4".

DIAGRAM B

G = hipline at side seam.
Pivot E to F from G.
Connect F to G to finish new side seam.
Connect B to D and C to D to finish pants.

Note: Use the same procedure for stylized pants.

DIAGRAM—Pants Waist Dart

DIAGRAM A

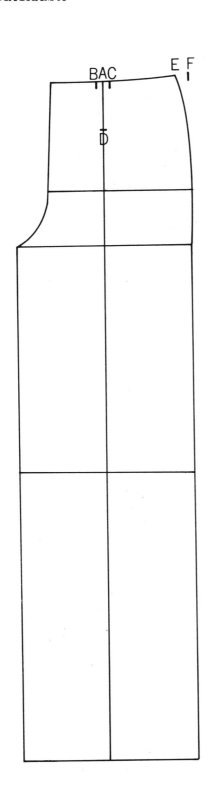

DIAGRAM B

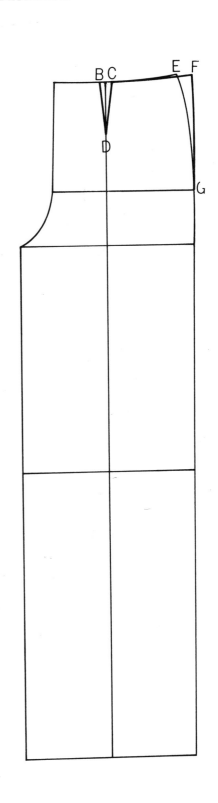

PLEATED PANTS

Outline front pants sloper.
Pleats toward side seam.

DIAGRAM A

A to C = grainline.
Slash or pivot A to B 1 1/2".
Connect B to C.

DIAGRAM B

B to D = pleat length according to design.

Note: Use the same procedure for stylized pants.

33

DIAGRAM—Pleated Pants

DIAGRAM A

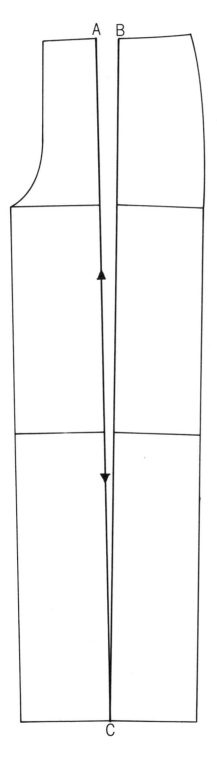

DIAGRAM B

DOUBLE PLEATED PANTS

Outline front pants sloper.
Pleats toward center front.

DIAGRAM A

Pivot or slash A to B 1 1/2".
B to C = grain line.

DIAGRAM B

First Pleat
A to B = 1 1/2".
A to D = pleat length according to design.

Second Pleat

E to F = 3/4".
G to H = 3/4".
I = crotchline at side seam.
Connect H to I.

Note: Use the same procedure for stylized pants.

DIAGRAM—Double Pleated Pants

DIAGRAM A

DIAGRAM B

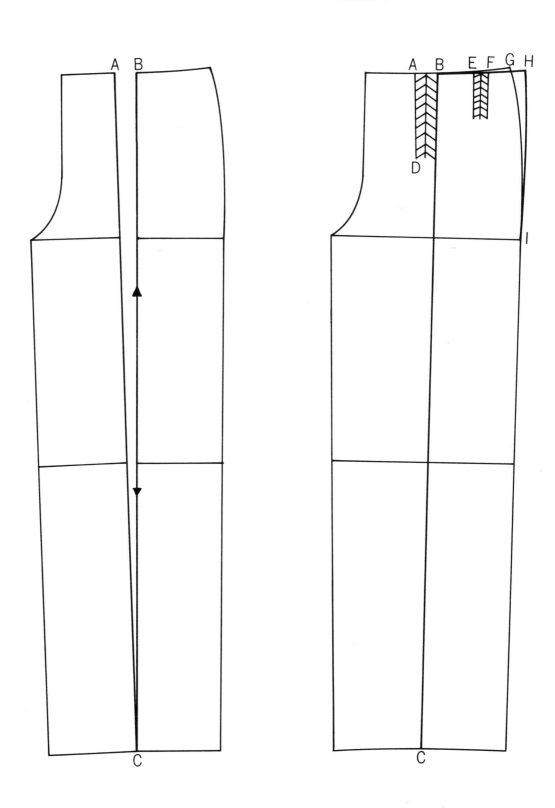

BASIC PANTS

Circumference of hem = 20".

Outline basic pants sloper including grain line, hip line, crotch line, and knee line.

Front Pants
A = grain line at hem.
A to B = 4 1/2".
A to C = 4 1/2".
D = intersection of crotch and inseam.
D to E = 1".
Connect B to E with straight line as a guide.
F = knee.
Connect F to D with hip curve ruler.
G = grain line at knee.
G to H = G to F.
I = hip line at side seam.
Connect C to H with straight line.
Connect H to I with straight line to finish front pants.

Back Pants
J = grain line at hem.
J to K = A to B + 1".
J to L = A to C + 1".
M = knee.
M to N = G to F + 1".
M to O = G to H + 1".
P = hip line at side seam.
Q = intersection of crotch and inseam.
Connect K to N with straight line.
Connect N to P with straight line.
Connect L to O with straight line.
Connect O to Q with hip curve ruler to finish back pants.

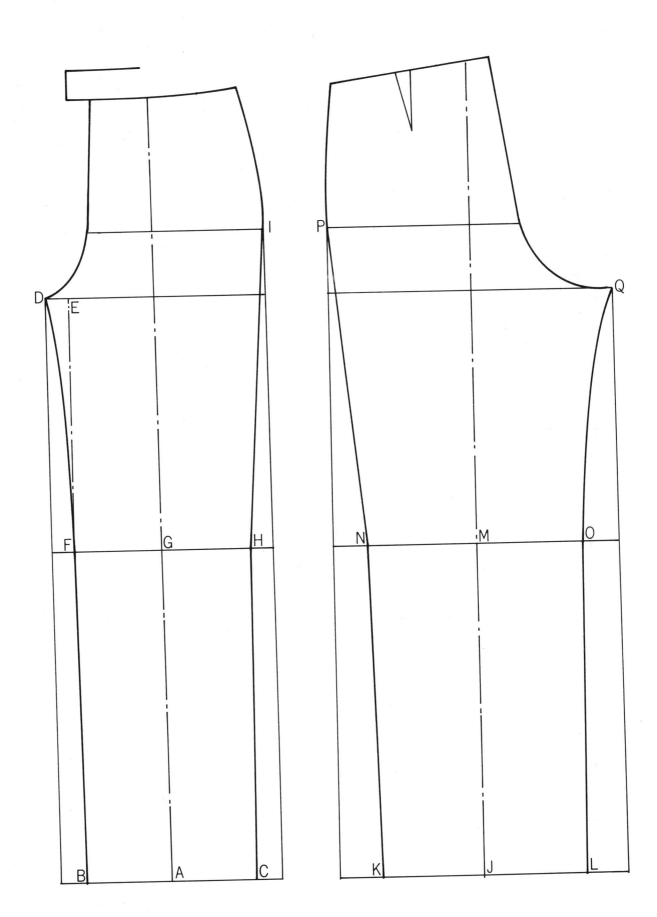

CUFFED BASIC PANTS WITH PATCH POCKET

Outline basic pants sloper.

Front Pants

A to B = 4 3/4".
A to C = 4 3/4".
B to C = 3 1/2" for cuff.
C to E = 3 1/2" for cuff.
A to F = 1 3/4".
G = knee.
H to I = 1".
G to J = G to I.
Connect D to I with straight line.
I to L = hip curve.
Connect E to J with straight line.
Connect J to K with straight line to finish front pants.

Back Pants

M to N = A to B + 1".
M to O = A to C + 1".
N to Q = 3 1/2" for cuff.
O to P = 3 1/2'. for cuff.
M to R = 1 3/4".
S = knee.
S to T = G to I + 1".
S to U = G to J + 1".
Connect Q to T with straight line.
Connect T to W with straight line.
Connect P to U with straight line.
Connect U to V with hip curve ruler to finish back
   pants.

Pocket

1 to 2 = 2 1/2".
2 to 3 = 1/2".
3 to 4 = 6".
4 to 5 = 3/8".
Connect 3 to 5.
3 to 6 = 6 1/2" parallel to crease line.
6 to 7 = 6".
Connect 3 to 6, 6 to 7, and 7 to 5 to finish pocket.

DIAGRAM—Cuffed Basic Pants with Patch Pocket

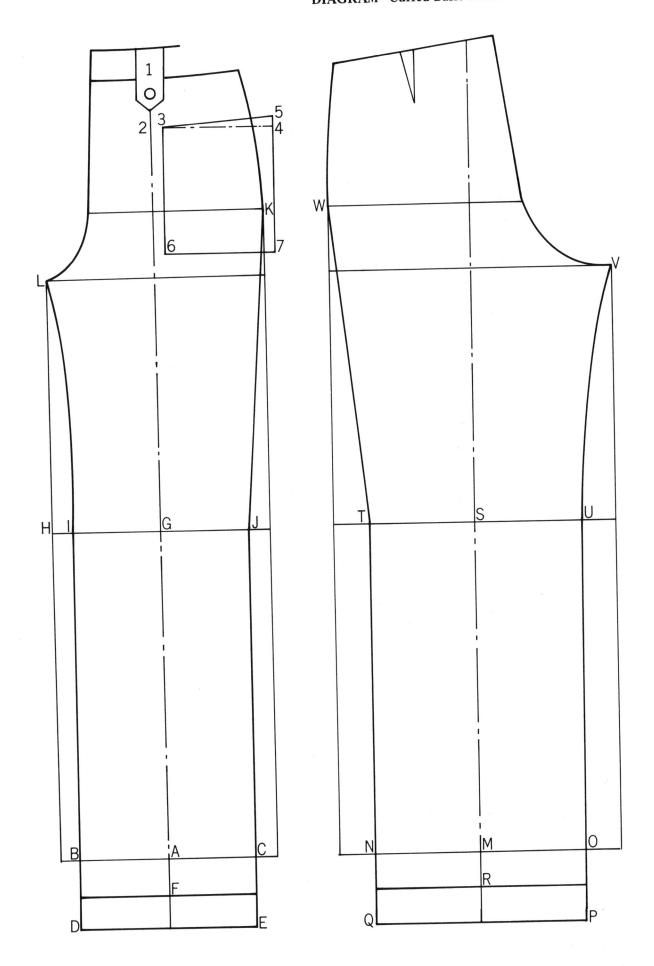

BASIC PANTS WITH DIAGONAL POCKET

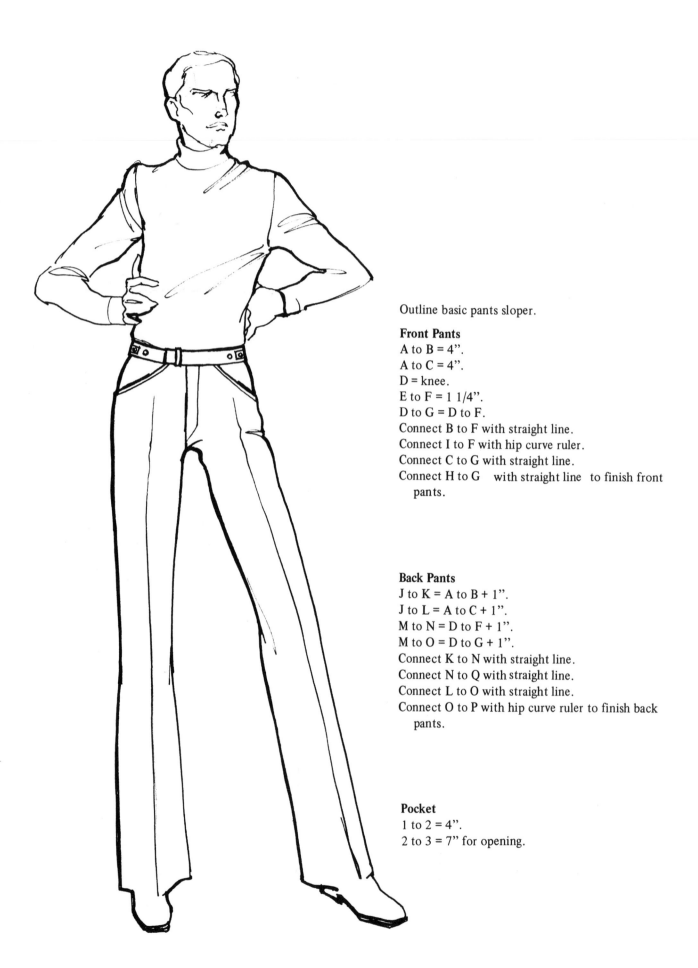

Outline basic pants sloper.

Front Pants
A to B = 4".
A to C = 4".
D = knee.
E to F = 1 1/4".
D to G = D to F.
Connect B to F with straight line.
Connect I to F with hip curve ruler.
Connect C to G with straight line.
Connect H to G   with straight line to finish front
   pants.

Back Pants
J to K = A to B + 1".
J to L = A to C + 1".
M to N = D to F + 1".
M to O = D to G + 1".
Connect K to N with straight line.
Connect N to Q with straight line.
Connect L to O with straight line.
Connect O to P with hip curve ruler to finish back
   pants.

Pocket
1 to 2 = 4".
2 to 3 = 7" for opening.

DIAGRAM—Basic Pants with Diagonal Pocket

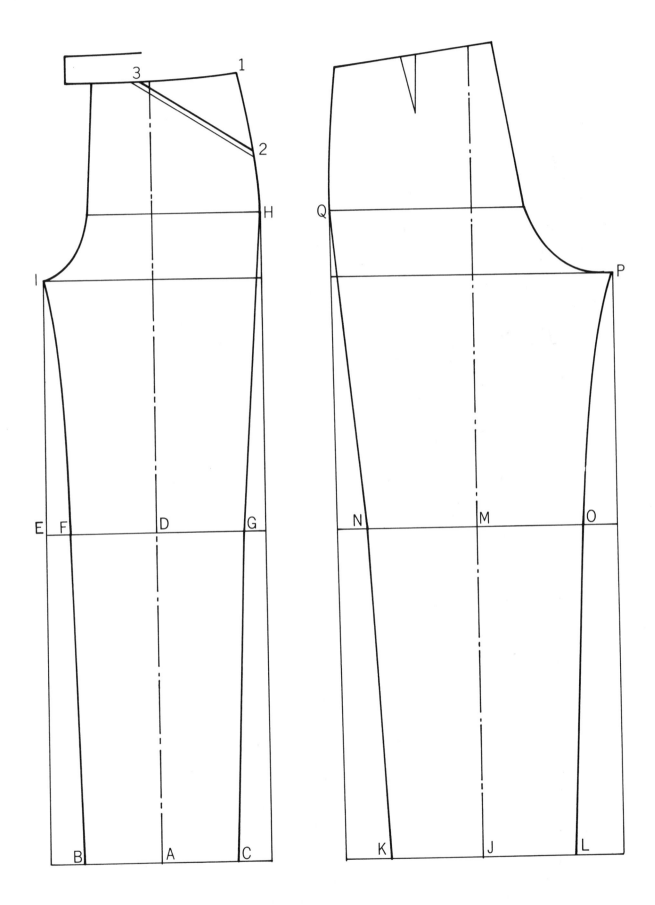

BASIC STRAIGHT PANTS

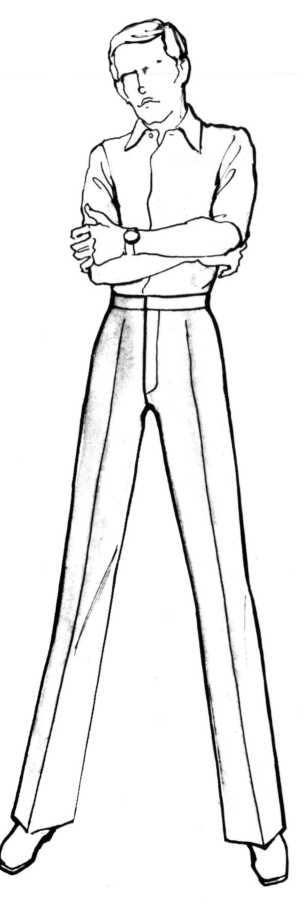

Outline basic pants sloper.

Front Pants
A = 1/2 B to C.
D to E = 1 1/2".
A to F = A to E.
G to H = A to E.
G to I = A to F.
Connect H to E with straight line.
Connect E to K with hip curve ruler.
Connect I to F with straight line.
Connect F to J with hip curve to finish front pants.

Back Pants
L = 1/2 M to N.
L to O = A to E + 1".
L to P = A to F + 1".
Q to R = L to O.
Q to S = L to P.
Connect R to O with straight line.
Connect O to U with hip curve ruler.
Connect S to P with straight line.
Connect P to T with hip curve ruler to finish back pants.

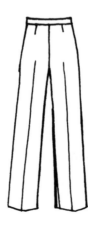

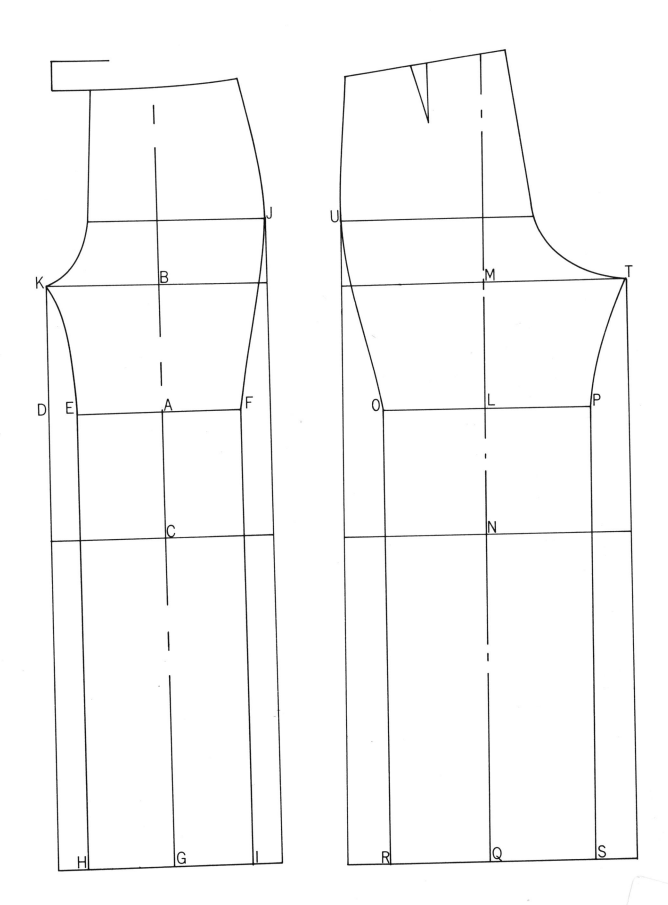

STRAIGHT PANTS WITH DOUBLE PIPING POCKET

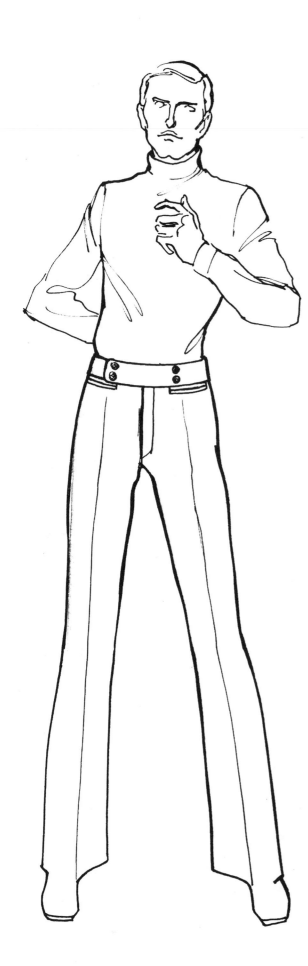

Outline basic pants sloper.

Front Pants
A to B = 4 1/2".
B to C = 4 1/2".
D = 1/2 E to F.
G to H = 1 1/4".
D to I = D to H.
Connect B to H with straight line.
Connect H to K with hip curve ruler.
Connect C to I with straight line.
Connect I to J with hip curve ruler to finish front pants.

Back Pants
L to M = A to B + 1".
L to N = A to C + 1".
O = 1/2 P to Q.
O to R = D to H + 1".
O to S = D to I + 1".
Connect M to R with straight line.
Connect R to U with hip curve ruler.
Connect N to S with straight line.
Connect S to T with hip curve ruler to finish back pants.

Pocket
1 to 2 = 3/4".
2 to 3 = 5" for opening.
Width of piping = 3/8" or according to design.

DIAGRAM–Straight Pants with Double Piping Pocket

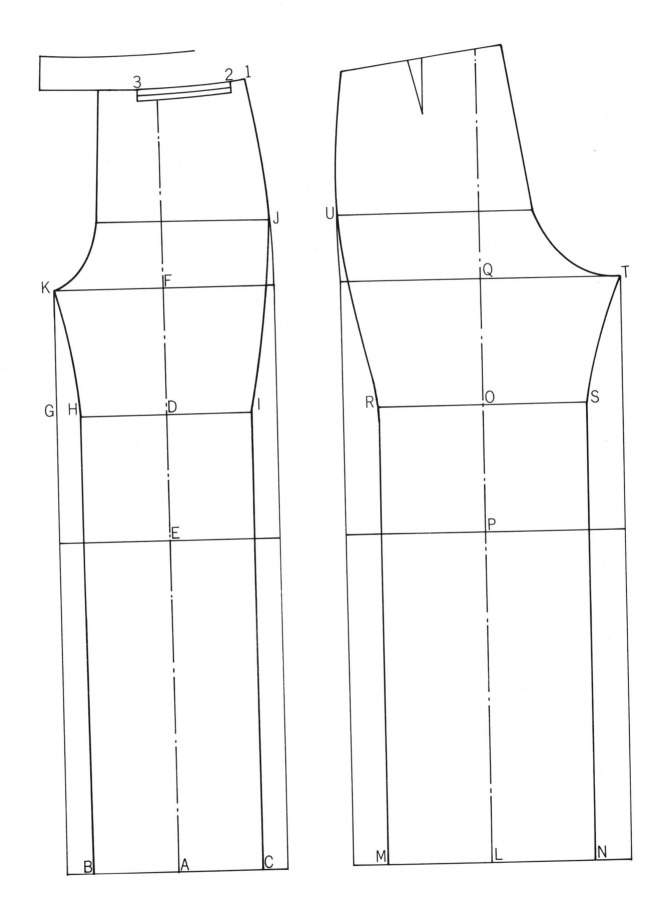

CUFFED STRAIGHT PANTS WITH VERTICAL PIPING POCKET

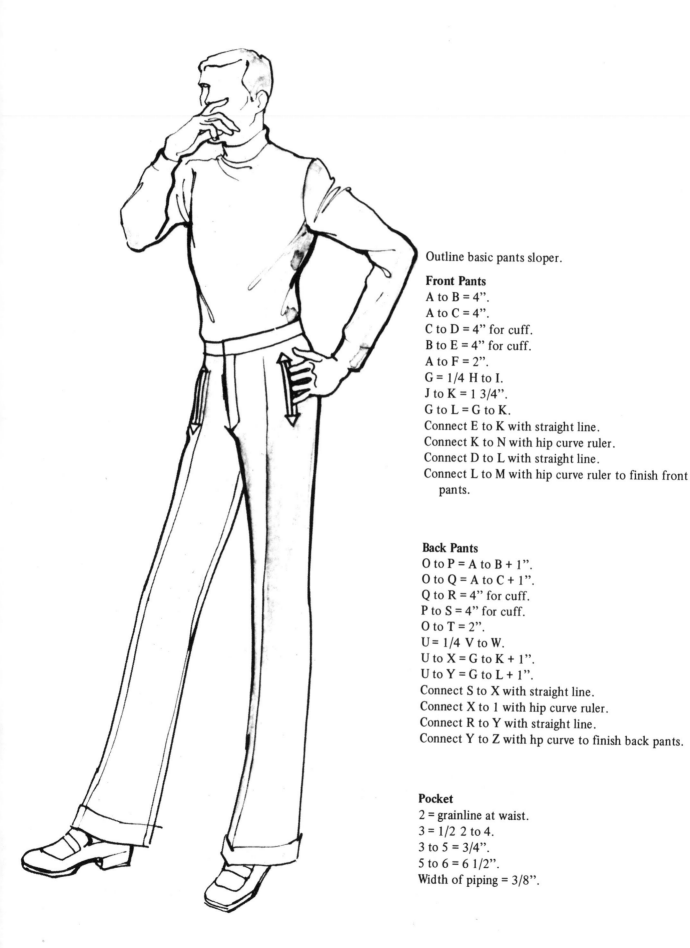

Outline basic pants sloper.

Front Pants
A to B = 4".
A to C = 4".
C to D = 4" for cuff.
B to E = 4" for cuff.
A to F = 2".
G = 1/4 H to I.
J to K = 1 3/4".
G to L = G to K.
Connect E to K with straight line.
Connect K to N with hip curve ruler.
Connect D to L with straight line.
Connect L to M with hip curve ruler to finish front
　　pants.

Back Pants
O to P = A to B + 1".
O to Q = A to C + 1".
Q to R = 4" for cuff.
P to S = 4" for cuff.
O to T = 2".
U = 1/4 V to W.
U to X = G to K + 1".
U to Y = G to L + 1".
Connect S to X with straight line.
Connect X to 1 with hip curve ruler.
Connect R to Y with straight line.
Connect Y to Z with hp curve to finish back pants.

Pocket
2 = grainline at waist.
3 = 1/2 2 to 4.
3 to 5 = 3/4".
5 to 6 = 6 1/2".
Width of piping = 3/8".

DIAGRAM—Cuffed Straight Pants with Vertical Piping Pocket

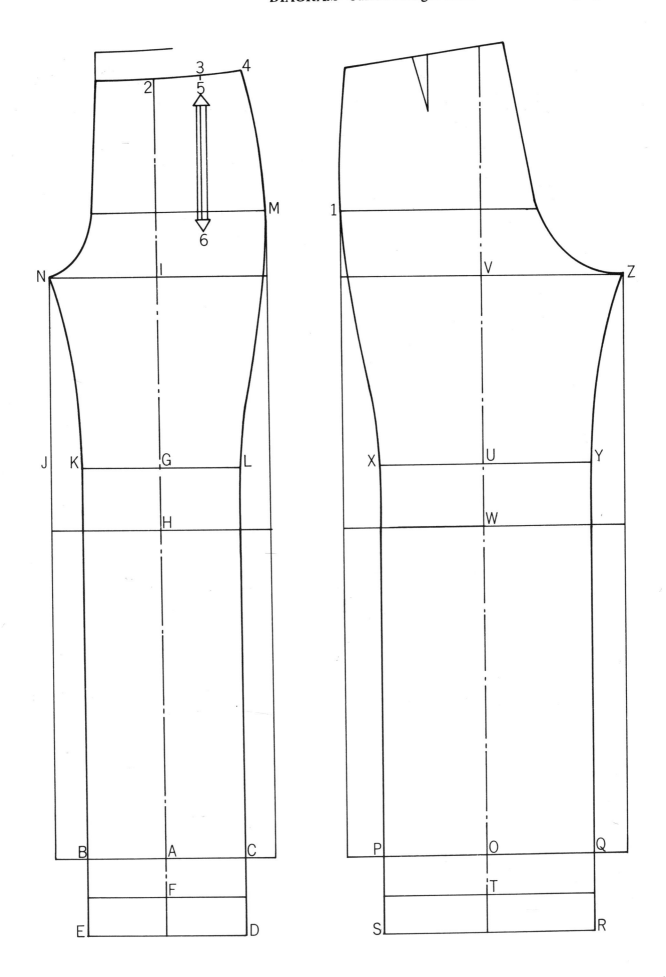

STRAIGHT PANTS VARIATION WITH WELT POCKET

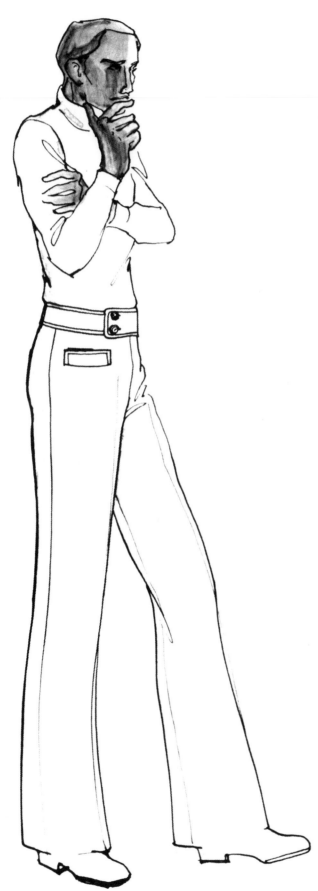

Outline basic pants sloper.

Front Pants
A to B = 4 3/4".
A to C = 4 3/4".
D = 1/4 E to F.
G to H = 1".
D to I = D to H.
Connect B to H with straight line.
Connect H to J with hip curve ruler.
Connect C to I with straight line.
Connect I to K with hip curve ruler to finish front pants.

Back Pants
L to M = A to B + 1".
L to N = A to C + 1".
O = 1/4 P to Q.
O to R = D to H + 1".
O to S = D to I + 1".
Connect M to R with straight line.
Connect R to U with hip curve ruler.
Connect N to S with straight line.
Connect S to T with hip curve ruler to finish back pants.

Pocket
1 to 2 = 3/4".
2 to 3 = 1 1/2".
3 to 4 = 5" for opening.
3 to 5 = 1 1/2" for welt width.
4 to 6 = 1 1/2".
Connect 3 to 4, 4 to 6, 6 to 5, and 5 to 3 to finish pocket.

DIAGRAM—Straight Pants Variation with Welt Pocket

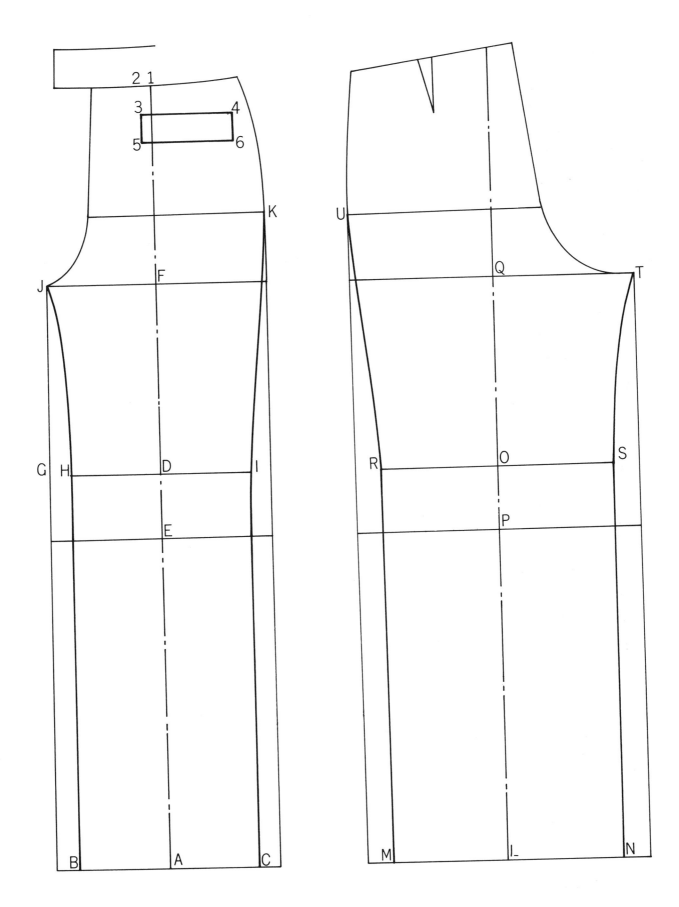

FLARE PANTS

Outline basic pants sloper.

Front Pants
A to B = 5 3/4".
A to C = 5 3/4".
D = 1/4 E to F.
G to H = 1 1/2".
D to I = D to H.
H and I = flare point.
Flare point can be higher or lower according to design.
Connect B to H with straight line.
Connect H to J with hip curve ruler.
Connect C to I with straight line.
Connect I to K with hip curve ruler to finish front pants.

Back Pants
L to M = A to B + 1".
L to N = A to C + 1".
O = 1/4 P to Q.
O to R = D to H + 1".
O to S = D to I + 1".
Connect M to R with straight line.
Connect R to U with hip curve ruler.
Connect N to S with straight line.
Connect S to T with hip curve ruler to finish back pants.

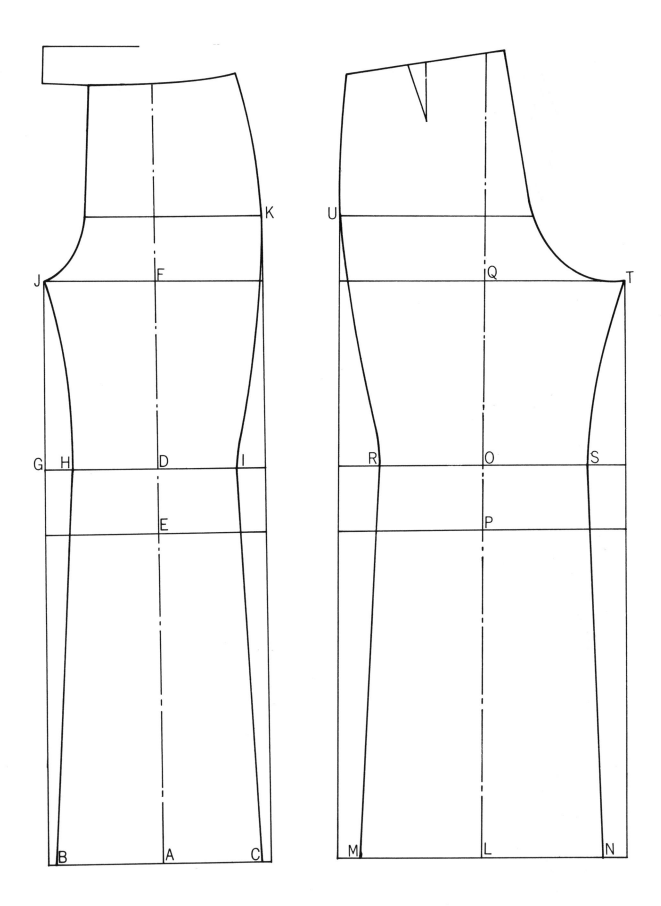

PLEATED FLARE PANTS A

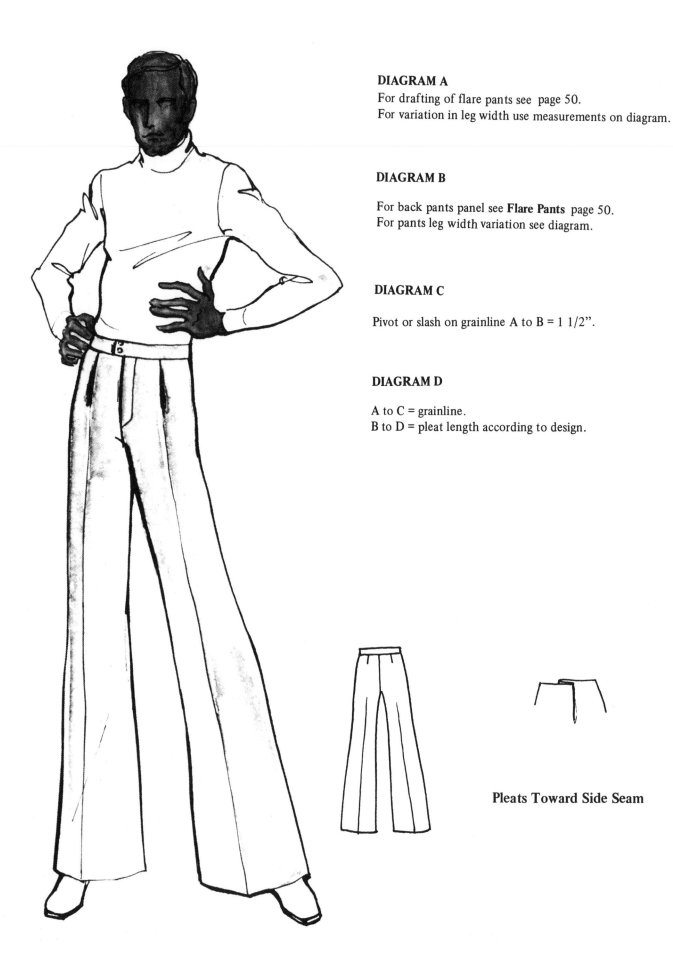

DIAGRAM A

For drafting of flare pants see page 50.
For variation in leg width use measurements on diagram.

DIAGRAM B

For back pants panel see **Flare Pants** page 50.
For pants leg width variation see diagram.

DIAGRAM C

Pivot or slash on grainline A to B = 1 1/2".

DIAGRAM D

A to C = grainline.
B to D = pleat length according to design.

Pleats Toward Side Seam

A

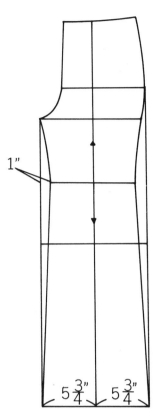

1"

5$\frac{3}{4}$"   5$\frac{3}{4}$"

B

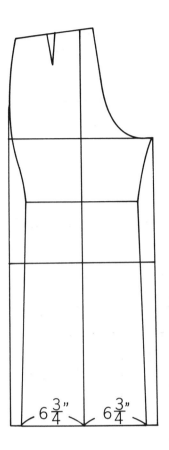

6$\frac{3}{4}$"   6$\frac{3}{4}$"

C

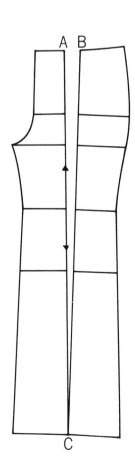

A B

C

D

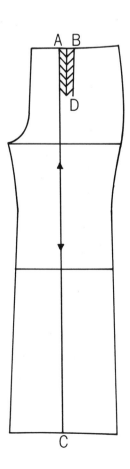

A B

D

C

PLEATED FLARE PANTS B

Outline your pants sloper.

DIAGRAM A

For drafting flare pants see page 50.
For variation in leg width use measurements on diagram.

DIAGRAM B

For back pants panel see **Flare Pants** page 50.
For pants leg width variation see diagram.

DIAGRAM C

Pivot or slash grain line A to B = 1 1/2".

DIAGRAM D

B to C = grainline.
A to D = pleat length according to design.

Pleats Toward Center Front

DIAGRAM—Pleated Flare Pants

DIAGRAM A

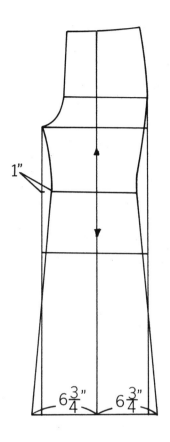

1"

$6\frac{3}{4}$" $6\frac{3}{4}$"

DIAGRAM B

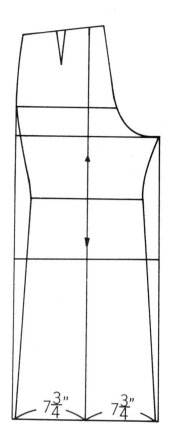

$7\frac{3}{4}$" $7\frac{3}{4}$"

DIAGRAM C

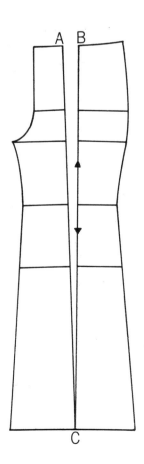

A B

C

DIAGRAM D

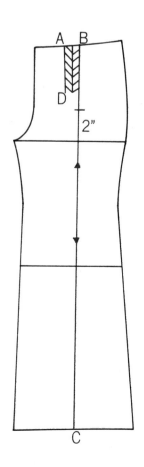

A B

D

2"

C

CASUAL SHORTS

Outline basic pants sloper.

Front Pants
A = 1/2 B to C.
C = knee.
A to D = 1".
E to F = 1 3/4".
D to G = D to F.
Connect F to H with hip curve ruler.
Connect G to I with hip curve ruler to finish front
    pants.

Back Pants
J = 1/2 K to L.
J to M = 1".
M to N = D to F + 1".
M to O = D to G + 1".
Connect O to P with hip curve ruler.
Connect N to Q with hip curve ruler to finish back
    pants.

Pocket
R = side seam at waist.
R to S = 5".
S to T = 7".
U = grainline at waist.
U to V = 1 1/4".
Connect V to S with sleigh curve ruler.
Connect U to B to T according to design to
    finish pocket.

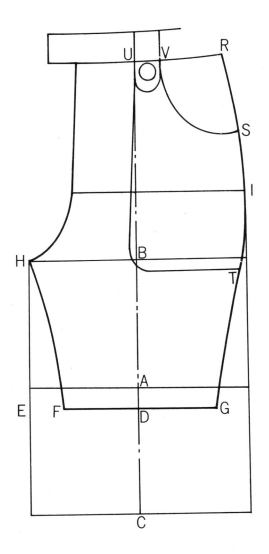

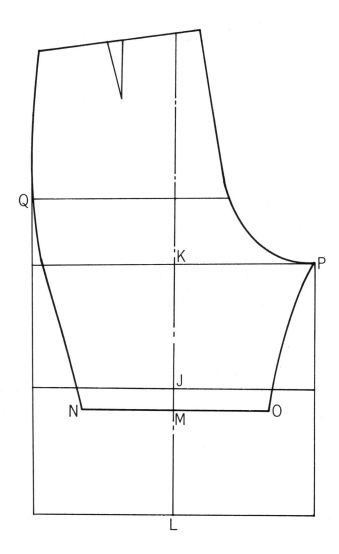

WALKING SHORTS

Outline basic pants sloper.

Front Pants
A = knee.
A to B = 1".
C to D = 1 3/4".
B to E = B to D.
B to F = 1 1/2" for cuff.
F to G = 1 1/2" for cuff.
Connect D to H with hip curve ruler.
Connect E to I with hip curve ruler to finish front pants.

Back Pants
J = knee.
J to K = 1".
K to L = B to D + 1".
K to M = K to L.
K to N = 1 1/2" for cuff.
N to O = 1 1/2" for cuff.
Connect M to P with hip curve ruler.
Connect L to Q with hip curve ruler to finish back pants.

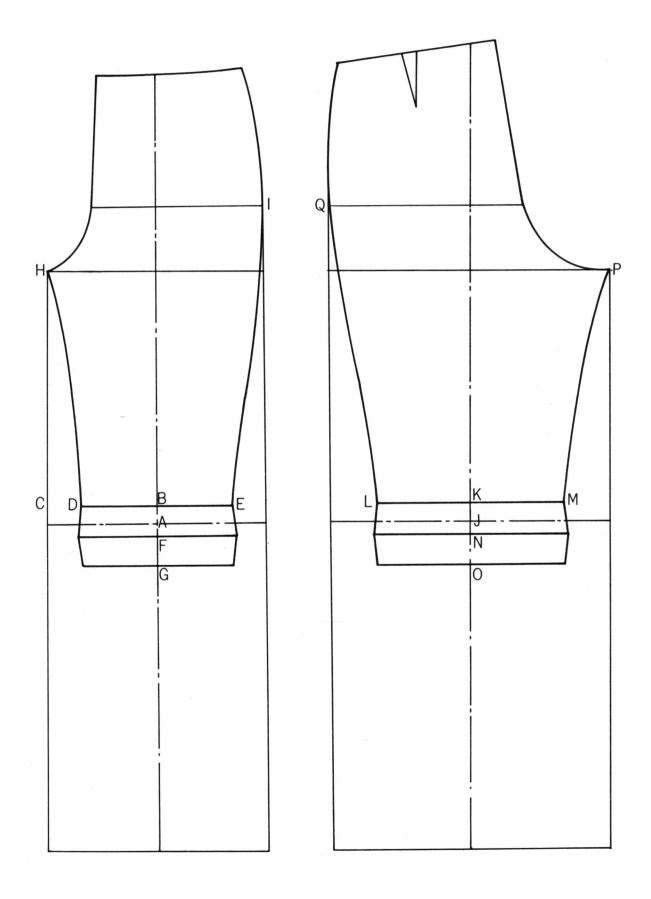

SHORT KNICKERS

Outline basic pants sloper.

Front Pants
A = 1/2 B to C.
B to D = 3".
E to F = 1 1/2".
A to G = A to F.
H to I = 1".
D to J = D to I.
Connect I to F with straight line.
Connect F to L with hip curve ruler.
Connect J to G with straight line.
Connect G to K with hip curve ruler.
Connect I to J to finish front pants.

Back Pants
M = 1/2 N to O.
N to P = 3".
M to Q = A to F + 1".
M to R = A to G + 1".
O to S = D to I + 1".
P to T = D to J + 1".
Connect S to Q with straight line.
Connect Q to V with hip curve ruler.
Connect T to R with straight line.
Connect R to U with hip curve ruler.
Connect S to T to finish back pants.

1 to 2 = knee measurement + 1" for extension.

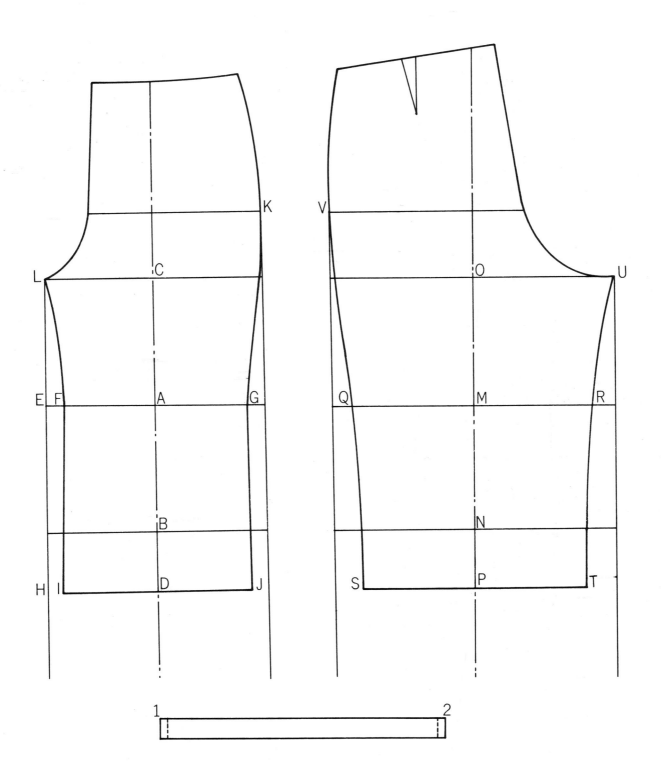

LONG KNICKERS

Outline basic pants sloper.

Front Pants
A = 1/2 B to C.
D = 1/2 C to E.
F to G = 3/4".
A to H = A to G.
D to I = 1/2 front leg width.
D to J = D to I.
Connect I to G with straight line.
Connect G to L with hip curve ruler.
Connect J to H with straight line.
Connect I to J to finish front pants.

Back Pants
M = 1/2 N to O.
P = 1/2 O to Q.
M to R = A to G + 1".
M to S = A to H + 1".
P to T = D to I + 1".
P to U = D to J + 1".
Connect T to R with straight line.
Connect R to W with hip curve ruler.
Connect U to S with straight line.
Connect S to V with hip curve ruler.
Connect T to U to finish back pants.

Hem Band
1" wide.
1 to 2 = calf measurement + 1/2" for ease + 1" for
  extension.

DIAGRAM—Long Knickers

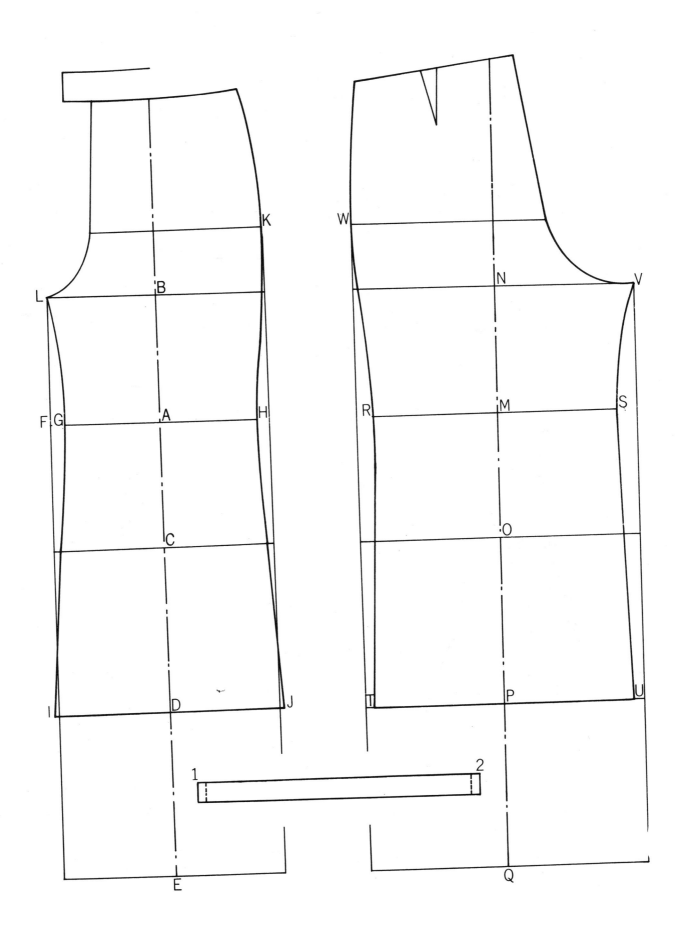

BASIC JACKET SLOPER

DIAGRAM A

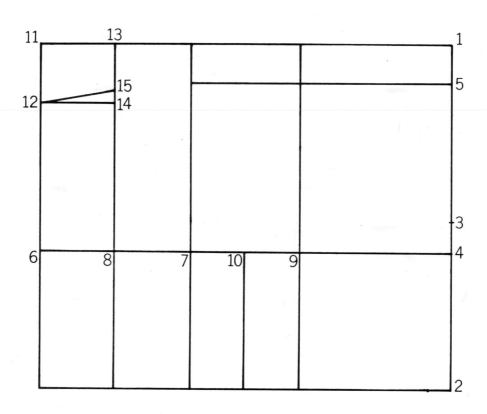

In order to draft Basic Jacket Sloper, the following measurements are needed:

1/2 = chest circumference + 3-1/2" for ease, center front to center back.
1/2 = front chest.
1/2 = shoulder blade.

See **Size Chart**, pages 6-7.

1 = back neck point.
1 to 2 = back waist length (center back).
2 = waist.
3 = 1/2 1 to 2.
4 = chest.
3 to 4 = 1-3/4".
1 to 5 = 1/5 1 to 4.
5 = shoulder guideline.
Square off from 1, 5, 4, and 2 toward left.
4 to 6 = 1/2 chest + 3-1/2" for ease.
6 to 7 = 1/2 front chest + 3/8".
8 = 1/2 6 to 7.
4 to 9 = 1/2 shoulder blade -1/4".
10 = 1/2 9 to 7 to establish side seam.
Square up and down from 6 to establish center front.
Square up and down from 8, 7, and 9.
Square down from 10 to waist.
11 to 12 = 11 to 13 -3/4".
Square off 12 to 14.
14 to 15 = 3/4".
Connect 12 to 15 with straight line.

BASIC JACKET SLOPER

DIAGRAM B

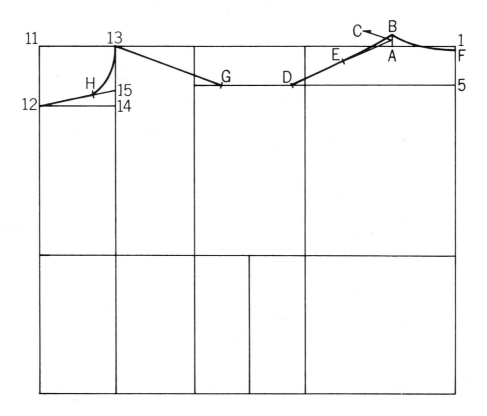

In order to draft neck and shoulder lines, the following measurement is needed:

Shoulder length.

See **Size Chart**, pages 6-7

Back
1 to A = 11 to 13 − 5/8".
A to B = back neck rise = 1/3 1 to A -1/4".
C = 1/2 A to B.
C to D = shoulder length -1/8".
Connect C to D with straight line as a guide.
E = 1/2 C to D.
Connect B to E with hip curve ruler, joining E to D to finish back shoulder.
1 to F = 1/8".
Connect B to F with sleigh curve ruler to finish back neckline.

Front
13 to G = B to D -3/8" to establish front shoulder length.
Connect 13 to G with straight line.
H = 1/3 15 to 12.
Connect 13 to H with sleigh curve ruler.
Connect H to 12 with straight line to finish neckline for jacket sloper.

BASIC JACKET SLOPER

DIAGRAM C

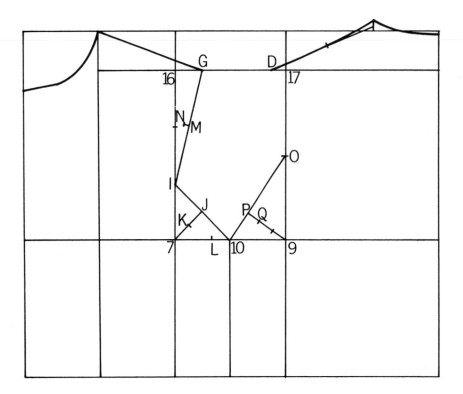

Front Armhole

Preparation:
I = Lower 1/3 16 to 7.
Connect I to 10; then connect I to G.
To locate J, square off along the line between I and 10 to 7.
K = 1/2 J to 7.
L = 1" from 10.
M = 1/2 G to I.
M to N = 1/4".

Back Armhole
Preparation:
O = 1/2 17 to 9.
Connect O to 10.
To locate P, square off along line between O and 10 to 9.
P to Q = 1/3 P to 9.

BASIC JACKET SLOPER

DIAGRAM D

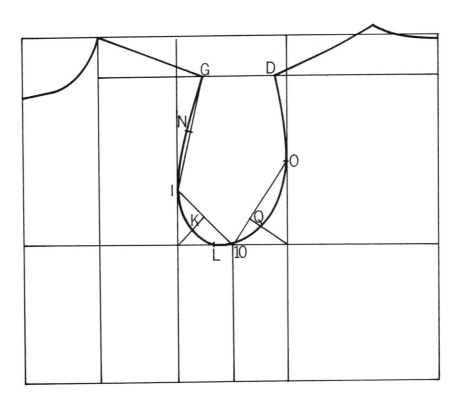

Completion of Armhole

Connect G to N to I with sleigh curve ruler.
Connect I to K to L to 10 to finish front armhole.
Connect O to Q to 10; then O to D with shallow part of sleigh curve ruler to finish
 back armhole.

JACKET SLOPER

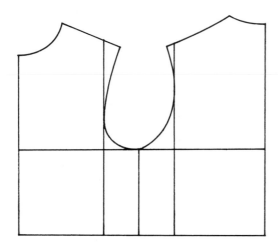

Outline basic sloper.

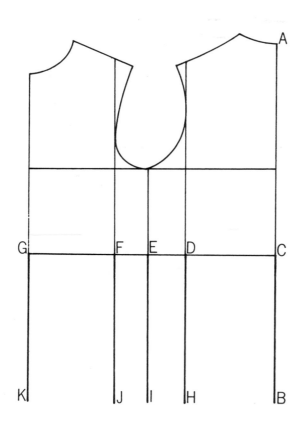

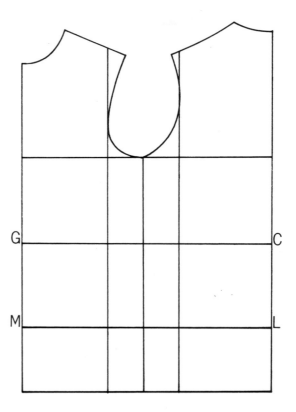

A to B = Jacket length.
C is at waistline.
Square off from D to H, E to I, F to J, G to K.
C to L = 8".
G to M = 8".

Connect L to M to finish hipline.
Connect B to K to finish hemline.

JACKET SLOPER PARTS

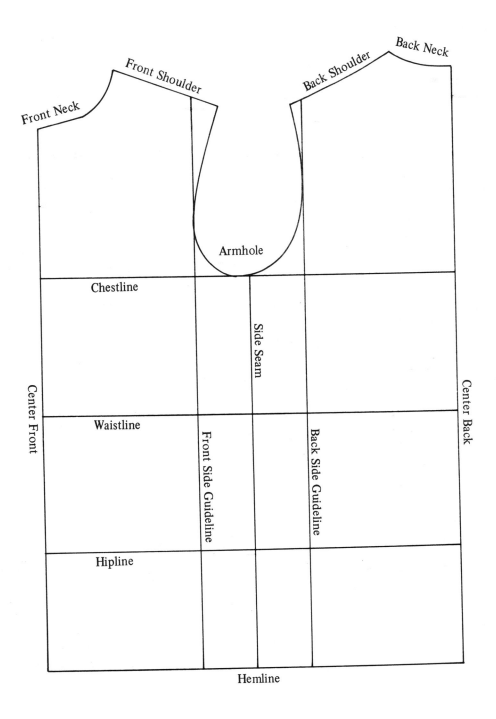

70

HIGH AND LOW ARMHOLES

DIAGRAM A

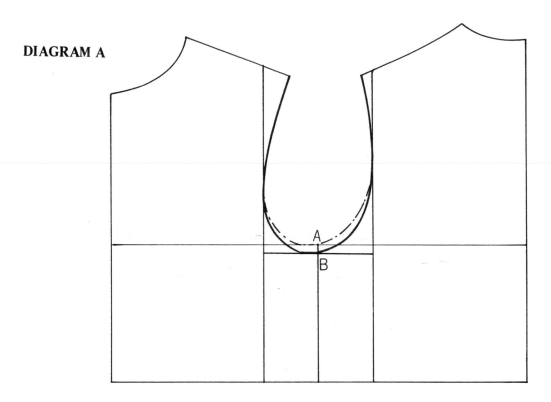

Armhole can be dropped according to design from original sloper.

Example: A to B = 1/2".

DIAGRAM B

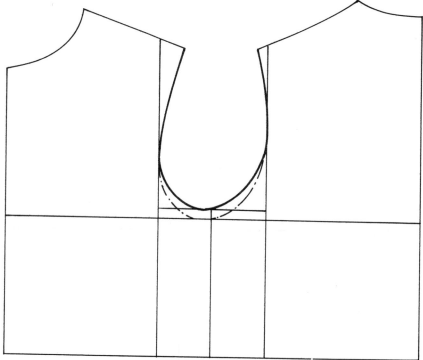

Armhole can be raised 1/2" to 1" according to design from original sloper.

SHIFTING SHOULDER LINE

DIAGRAM A

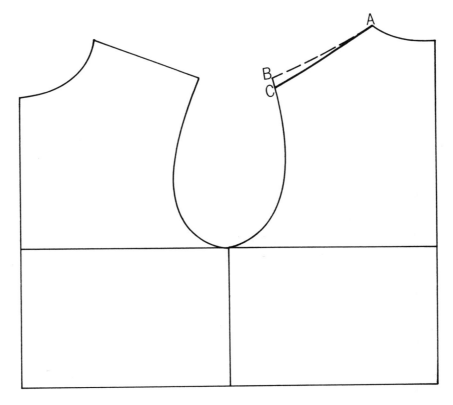

Back Shoulder
A = shoulder at neck.
B = shoulder at armhole.
B to C = 1/2".
Connect C to A with hip curve ruler and remove line A to B to C for new shoulder line A to C

DIAGRAM B

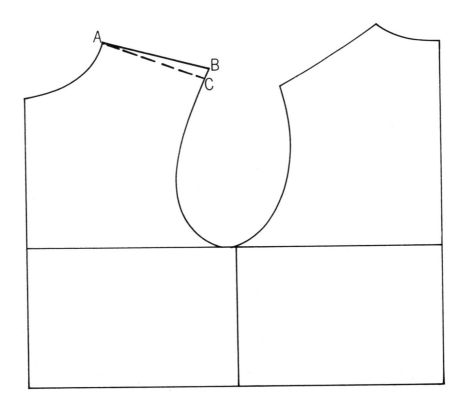

Front Shoulder
Add to the front shoulder the amount removed from the back shoulder.

CARDIGAN JACKET

Outline your sloper with jacket length.

Back Panel

A = 1/2 neck to chest.

B to C = 1".

D to E = 1".

Connect A to C and C to E with a straight line to finish
   center back.

F = side seam at chest line.

G to H = 1/4".

I to J = 1/2".

Connect F to H with hip curve ruler.

Connect H to J with straight line.

Front Panel

Side seam F to K = 3/4".

G to L = 1 1/4".

Connect K to L with hip curve ruler.

Connect L to I with straight line.

M to N = 3/4" extension.

O = neck point.

O to P = 1/4".

P to Q = 1/2".

Q to R = 3/4".

Connect Q to M with shallow curve to finish new center front.

Connect R to N with same curve as Q to M

S to T = 3/4".

T to U = 1/2".

Connect N to U with straight line.

W = 1/2 S to V.

Square off from U to W.

Connect W to I with shallow curve.

Connect new neckline X to Q.

Square off from point Q to R.

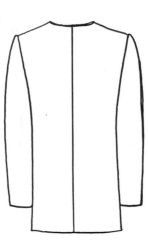

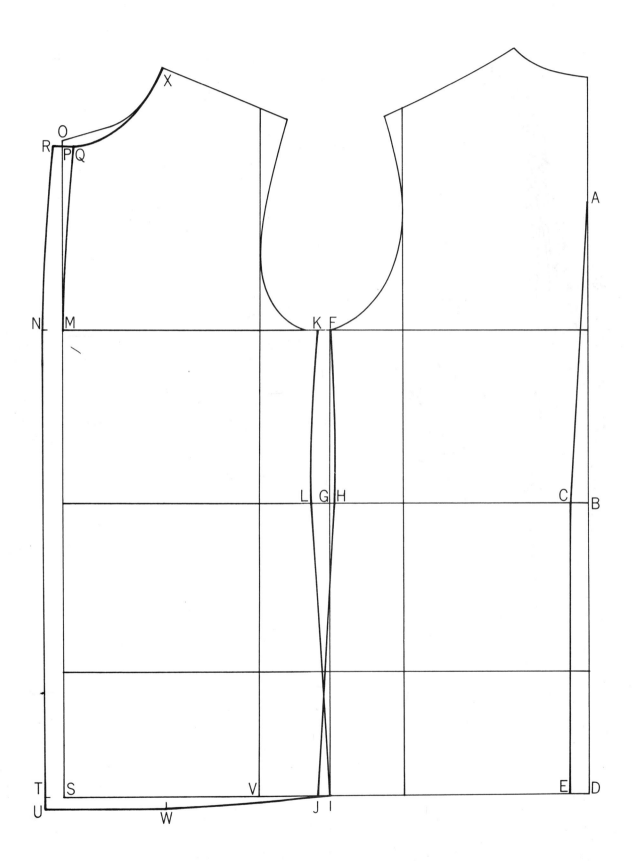

74

WORKMEN'S JACKET

Outline your sloper with jacket length.

Back Panel
A = 1/2 neck to chest.
B to C = 1".
D to E = 1".
Connect A to C, C to E with straight line to finish center back.
F = 1/3 G to H.
Square down from F to I.
J is at waist.
F to K = 1/4".
J to L = 1/2".
I to M = 1/4" or 1/2".
Connect K to L with hip curve ruler.
Connect L to M with straight line to finish back panel.

Front Panel
F to N = 1/4".
J to O = 1/2".
I to P = 1/4" or 1/2".
Connect N to O with same curve as K to L.
Connect O to P with straight line to finish side seam.
Q = chest line at center front.
Q to R = 3/4" for extension.
S to T = 3/4".
T to U = 1/2".
U to V = 3/4".
Connect U to Q with shallow curve to establish new center
  front.
Connect V to R with same curve as U to Q.
W to X 3/4" for extension.
X to Y = 1/2".
Connect R to X with straight line.
1 = 1/3 W to Z.
Square off Y to 1.
Y to 2 = 1".
3 to 6 = 3/4" for extension.
Connect 3 to 2 with straight line as a guide.
Connect 3 to 1 with curved line using both hip and sleigh
  curve rulers.
Connect 1 to P with shallow curve.
4 = shoulder at neck point.
Connect new neckline from 4 to U.
Square off from U to V.
5 = 1/2 6 to 7.
5 to 8 = 1/2".

9 = 1/2 5 to 8.
Square up from 9 to chest at 10.
Square down from 9 to 11 for 4".
Connect 10 to 5 to 11.
Connect 10 to 8 to 11 to finish
  waist dart.

Pocket, see pages 132-134.
Collar, see page 180.
Buttonhole, see page 128.

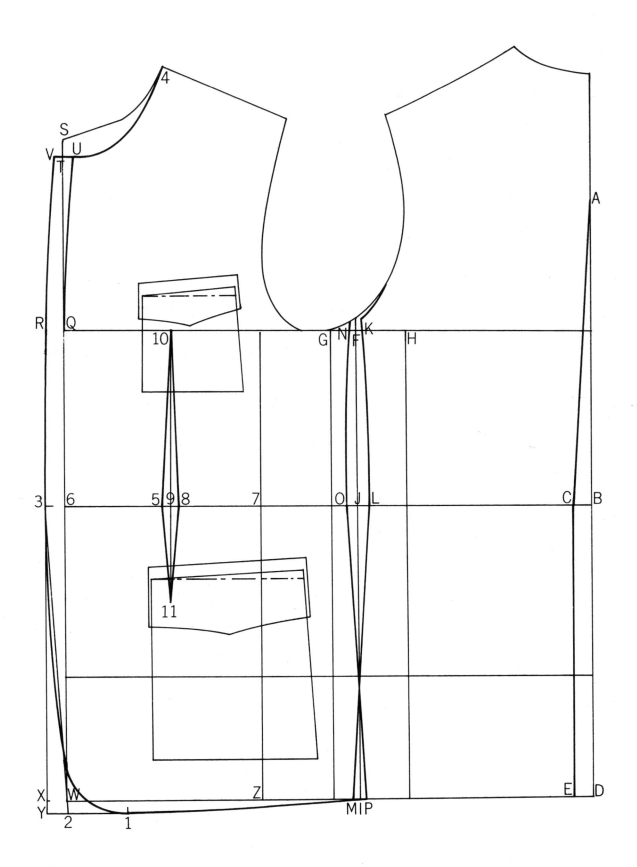

BUTTONED CARDIGAN JACKET WITH PATCH POCKET

Outline your sloper with jacket length

Back Panel
A = 1/2 neck to chest.
B to C = 3/4".
D to E = 3/4".
F = 1/3 G to H.
Square down from point F to I as a guideline.
J is at waistline.
F to K = 1/4".
J to L = 1/2".
I to M = 1/4".
Connect K to L with hip curve ruler.
Connect L to M with straight line.

Back Dart
N = 1/3 O to C.
Square up from point N to P.
Square down from point N to Q.
N to R = 1/4".
N to S = 1/4".
Q to T = 1/4".
Q to U = 1/4".
Connect P to R to T.
Connect P to S to U to finish dart.

Front Panel
Side seam F to V = 1/4".
J to W = 1/2".
I to X = 1/4".
Connect V to W with same curve as K to L.
Connect W to X with straight line.
Y is chest at center front.
Y to Z = 3/4" extension.
1 = neck point.
1 to 2 = 3/4".
2 to 3 = 1/2".
3 to 4 = 3/4".
Connect 3 to Y with shallow curve.
Connect 4 to Z with same curve as 3 to Y.
19 is shoulder at neck point.
Connect new neckline 19 to 3.
Square off from point 3 to 4 to finish neckline.
5 is center front at hem.
5 to 6 = 3/4"
6 to 7 = 1/2".
Connect Z to 7.

8 = 1/2 5 to 9.
Square off from point 7 to 8.
7 to 10 = 1".
11 is at waist.
Connect 11 to 10 as guideline.
Connect front design line; use both hip and sleigh curve
    rulers.

Front Dart
12 = 1/2 13 to 18.
Square up from point 12 to 17.
Square down 3" from point 12 to 14.
12 to 15 = 1/4".
12 to 16 = 1/4".
Connect 17 to 15 to 14.
Connect 17 to 16 to 14 to finish jacket.

Pocket, see pages 132-134.

Buttonhole, see page 128.

DIAGRAM—Buttoned Cardigan Jacket with Patch Pocket

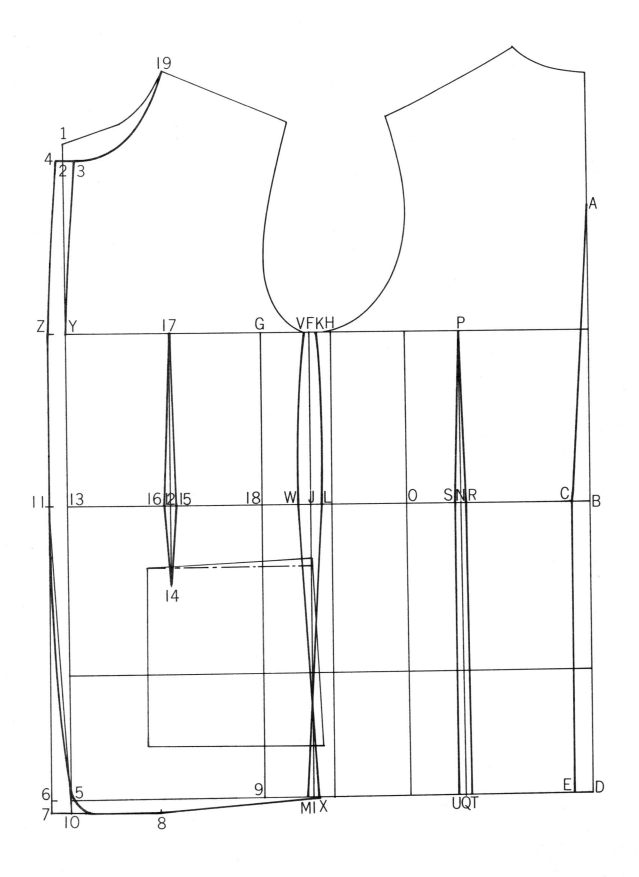

COLLARED CARDIGAN JACKET

Outline your sloper with jacket length.

Back Panel
A = 1/2 neck to chest.
B to C = 3/4".
D to E = 3/4".
Connect A to C to E to finish center back.
F = 3" up from chest line.
G to I = 3/4".
H to J = 3/4".
Connect F to I with hip curve ruler.
Connect I to J with straight line to finish back panel.

Back Dart
K = 1/2 I to C.
L = 1/2" from K.
M = 1/2 K to L.
Square down from M to N.
Square up from M to O.
N to P = 1/4".
N to Q = 1/4".
Connect O to K to P.
Connect O to L to Q to finish back dart.

Side Panel
G to R = 3/4".
H to S = 3/4".
T = 1/3 U to V.
Square down from T to W.
T to Y = 1/4".
X to 2 = 1/2".
W to 1 = 1/2".
Connect Y to 2 with hip curve ruler.
Connect 2 to 1 with straight line.

Front Panel
T to Z = 1/4".
X to 3 = 1/2".
W to 4 = 1/2".
Connect Z to 3 with hip curve ruler.
Connect 3 to 4 with straight line.

Front Dart
5 = 1/3 6 to U.
7 = 1/3 8 to 9.
10 = 4" below 7.
5 to 11 = 1/4".
7 to 12 = 1/2".
Connect 5 to 7 to 10 according to design line.
Connect 11 to 12 to 10 to finish front dart.
8 to 13 = 2".
13 to 14 = 3/4" extension.
15 = shoulder at neck point.
Connect 14 to 15 with straight line.

16 = 1/2 14 to 15.
16 to 17 = 1/4".
Connect 15 to 17 to 14 with hip curve ruler.
18 = center front at hem.
18 to 19 = 3/4".
19 to 20 = 1/2".
Connect 14 to 20.
21 = 1/2 18 to 22.
Square off from 20 to 21.
Connect 21 to S with shallow curve to finish jacket.

Pocket, see pages 132-124.
Collar, see page 178.
Buttonhole, see page 128.

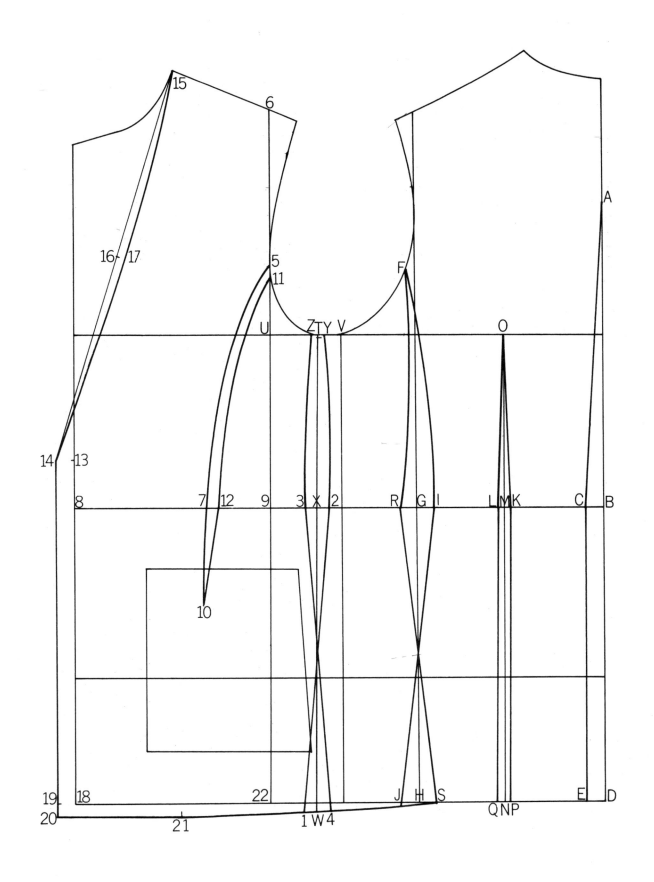

TENNIS JACKET

Outline your sloper with jacket length.

Back Panel

A = 1/2 neck to chest.
B to C = 3/4".
D to E = 3/4".
Connect A to C to E with straight line to finish center back.
F = 1/2 G to H.
I = 1/3 J to B.
Square down from I to K.
K to L = 3/4".
Connect F to I with curved line according to design.
Connect I to L with straight line to finish back panel.

Side Panel

I to M = 1 1/2".
Connect F to M with curved line.
Connect M to L with straight line.
N to O to P = side guideline.
O to Q = 3/8".
P to R = 1/2".
Connect N to Q with hip curve ruler.
Connect Q to R with straight line to finish side panel.

Front Panel

O to S = 3/8".
P to T = 1/2".
Connect N to S with same curve as N to Q.
Connect S to T with straight line.
U = 1/2 V to W.
U to X = 2 1/2".
Y = 2" above chest.
Y to Z = 1/2".
X to 1 = 2".
Connect Y to X with curved line according to design.
Connect Z to 1 with curved line to finish dart.
Note: Z is going out from original armhole.

Front Dart

Square up from U to 2.
Square down from U to 3.
U to 4 = 3/8".
U to 5 = 3/8".
3 to 6 = 3/8".
3 to 7 = 3/8".
Connect 2 to 4 to 6.
Connect 2 to 5 to 7 to finish front dart.

Front Tab

8 = center front at chest line.
8 to 9 = 1" extension.
8 to 10 = 1".
11 = center front at hem.
11 to 12 = 1".
12 to 13 = 1/2".
13 to 14 = 2".
Connect 9 to 13.
Connect 10 to 14.
15 = shoulder at neck point.
Connect 15 to 9 as a guide with straight line.
16 = 1/2 15 to 9.
16 to 17 = 1/4".
Connect 15 to 17 with hip curve ruler.
Connect 17 to 9 with hip curve and French curve.
Blend in 9 as shown in Diagram.
15 to 18 = 2".
Connect 18 to 10, using same curve as 15 to 9.
Blend in 10, the same as 9, to finish front tab.

Collar, see page 178.

Buttonhole, see page 128.

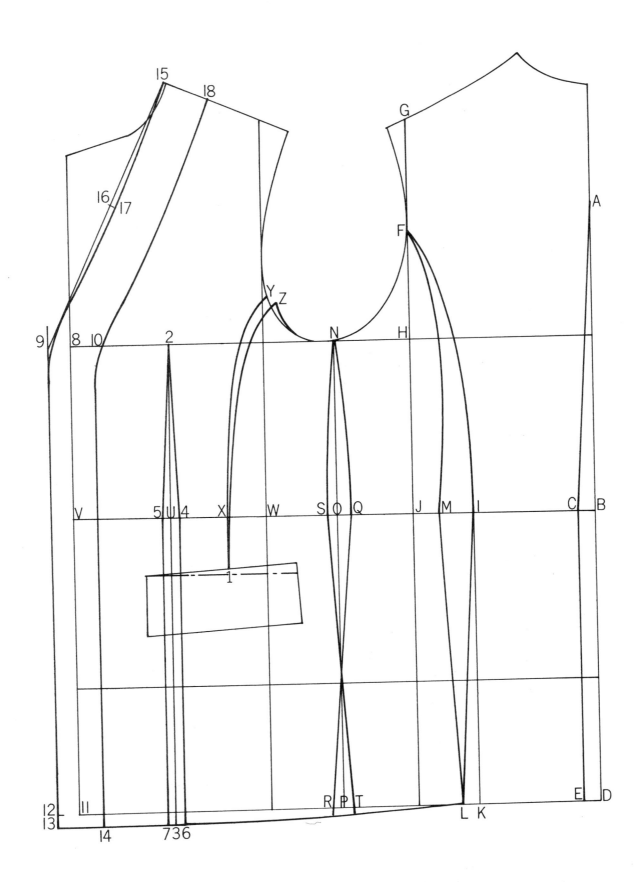

CASUAL JACKET DRAFTING PROCEDURE

Step 1

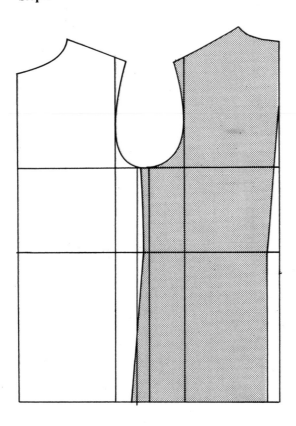

Step 2

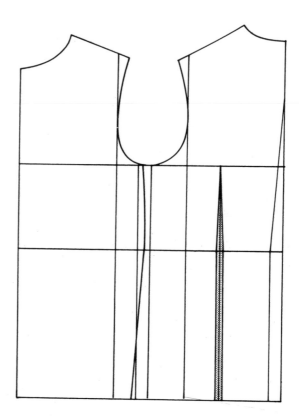

Step 3

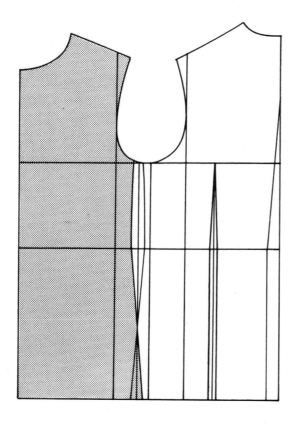

Step 4

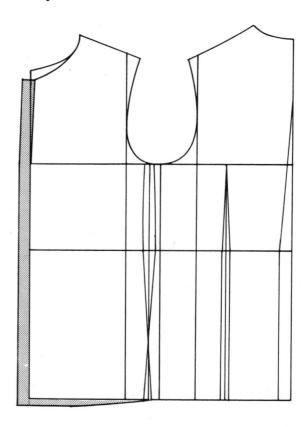

NOTES

SINGLE BREASTED BLAZER

Outline your sloper with jacket length.

Back Panel
A = 1/2 neck to chest.
B to C = 3/4".
D to E = 3/4".
Connect A to C to E.
F = 2 1/2" above chest.
G to I = 1 1/2".
H to J = 1/2".
Connect F to I with hip curve ruler.
Connect I to J with straight line to finish back panel.

Jacket Front
G to K = 1/4".
Connect F to K with hip curve ruler.
Connect K to J with straight line.
L = 1/3 M to N.
O = front side guideline at hem.
L to P = 1/4".
L to Q = 1/4".
R to S = 1/2".
R to T = 1/2".
R to U = 4".
Connect P to S with hip curve ruler (flat end).
Connect S to U with straight line.
Connect Q to T with same curve as P to S.
Connect T to U with straight line to finish side dart.
V = center front at waist.
V to W = 5".
W to X = 3/4".
Y = shoulder at neck.
Y to Z = collar stand.
Connect X to Z to establish roll line.

Square down from X to 1.
1 to 2 = 3/4".
Square off from 2 to 3.
3 = 1/2 of 1 to O.
Connect 3 to J with hip curve ruler to finish hemline.
2 to 5 = 1".
Connect 4 to 5 with straight line as a guide.
Connect 4 to 3 using both sleigh and hip curve rulers to finish
  front curve line.

Lapel
Extend neckline toward 6.
Square off from 7 to 6 for lapel width = 3-1/2" to 4".
Connect 6 to X with hip curve ruler using deeper curve toward
  X to finish lapel.

Front Waist Dart
8 = 1/2 of V to 9.
8 to 10 = 3-1/2".
11 = chest.
8 to 12 = 1/4".
Connect 11 to 12 to 10 with straight line.
Connect 11 to 8 to 11 with straight line to finish front dart.

Pocket, see pages 132-134.
Collar, see page 188.
Buttonhole, see page 130.

DIAGRAM—Single Breasted Blazer

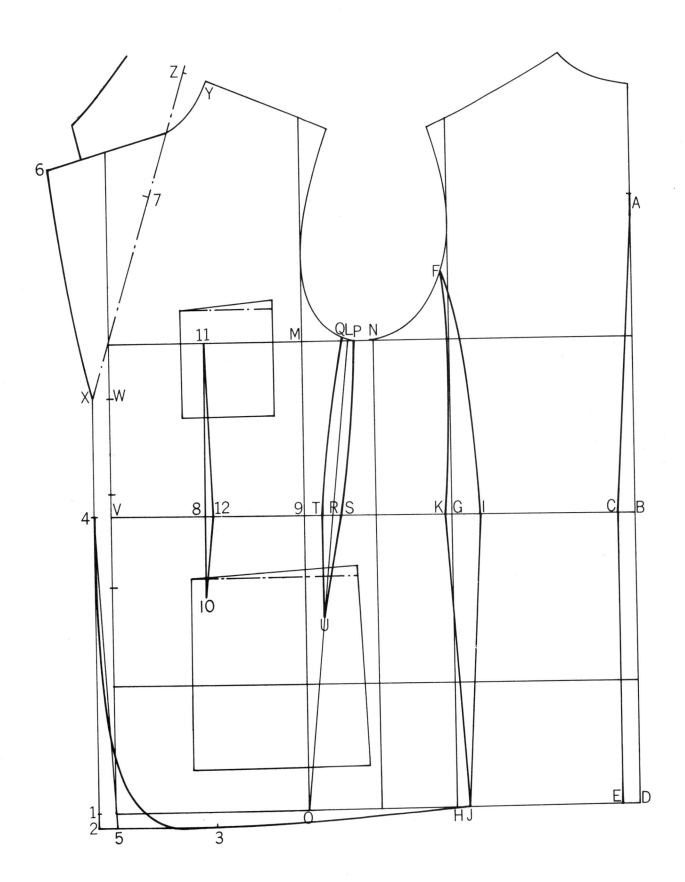

DOUBLE BREASTED BLAZER

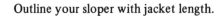

Outline your sloper with jacket length.

Back Panel
A = 1/2 neck to chest.
B to C = 3/4".
D to E = 3/4".
Connect A to C to D to finish center back.
F = 3" above chest line.
G to I = 1 1/4".
H to J = 1/2".
Connect F to I with hip curve ruler.
Connect I to J with straight line to finish back panel.

Front Panel
G to K = 1/4".
Connect F to K with shallow curve.
Connect K to J with straight line.

Side Dart
L = 1/3 M to N.
Connect L to P to O as a guideline.
L to Q = 1/4".
L to R = 1/4".
P to S = 1/2".
P to T = 1/2".
P to U = 4".
Connect Q to S with hip curve ruler.
Connect S to U with straight line.
Connect R to T with same curve as Q to S.
Connect T to U with straight line to finish dart.
V = center front on waistline.
V to W = 2".
W to X = 2 1/2" for extension.
Y = shoulder at neck point.
Y to Z = collar stand.
Connect X to Z to establish roll line.
Extend neckline toward 1.
Square off 2 to 1 to establish label width.
1 to 3 = 3".
Connect 3 to X with hip curve ruler; draw deeper curve toward X.
4 = 1/2 1 to 5.
Connect 3 to 4 to finish peaked lapel.
6 = center front on hemline.
6 to 7 = 2 1/2".
7 to 8 = 1/2".
9 = 1/2 6 to O.
Square off 8 to 9.
Connect 9 to J.

Front Dart
10 = 1/2 V to 11.
Square up from 10 to 12.
Square down from 10 to 13.
10 to 14 = 1/4".
Connect 12 to 14 to 13 to finish front panel.

Pocket, see pages 132-134.
Collar, see page 188.
Buttonhole, see page 130.

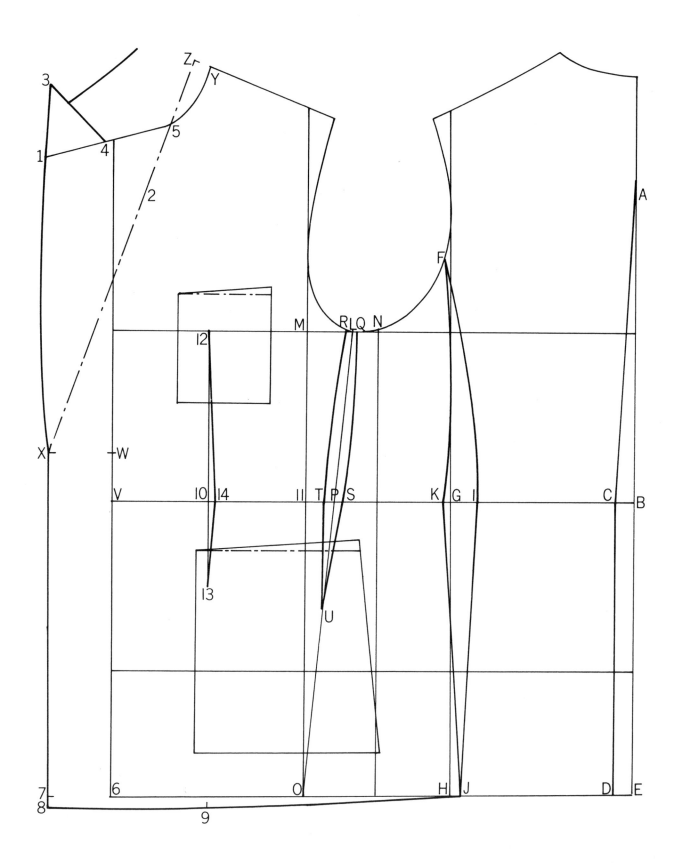

ONE-BUTTON SINGLE BREASTED ITALIAN CUT JACKET

Outline your sloper with jacket length.

Back Panel
A = 1/2 neck to chest line.
B to C = 1".
D to E = 1".
Connect A to C to E with straight line.
F = 2 1/2" above chest line.
G to I = 1 1/4".
H to J = 1/4".
Connect F to I with hip curve ruler.
Connect I to J with slight curve for more fit.

Side Panel
G to K = 1/4".
H to L = 1 1/4".
Connect F to K with **slight curve or straight edge.**
Connect K to L with straight line.
M = 1/3 N to O.
P = 1/3 R to Q.
M to T = 1/4".
S to U = 1/2".
P to V = 1/2".
Connect T to U with hip curve ruler.
Connect U to V with straight line to finish side panel.

Front Panel
M to W = 1/4".
S to X = 1/2".
P to Y = 1/2".
Connect W to X with hip curve ruler.
Connect X to Y with straight line.
Z = center front at waist line.
Z to 1 = 3/4" for extension.
2 = shoulder at neck.
2 to 3 = collar stand.
Extend neckline toward 5.
Square off 4 to 5 to establish lapel width.
5 to 6 = 2 1/2".
5 to 7 = 2 1/4".
Connect 6 to 1 with hip curve ruler.
Connect 6 to 7 with straight line to finish lapel.
8 to 9 = 3/4" for extension.
9 to 10 = 1/2".
10 to 11 = 2".
Connect 1 to 11 with straight line as a guide.
12 = 1/2 9 to R.
Connect 1 to 12 according to design.

Connect 12 to L with hip curve
ruler to finish jacket.

Pocket, see pages 132-134.
Collar, see page 188.
Buttonhole, see page 130.

DIAGRAM—One-Button Single Breasted Italian Cut Jacket

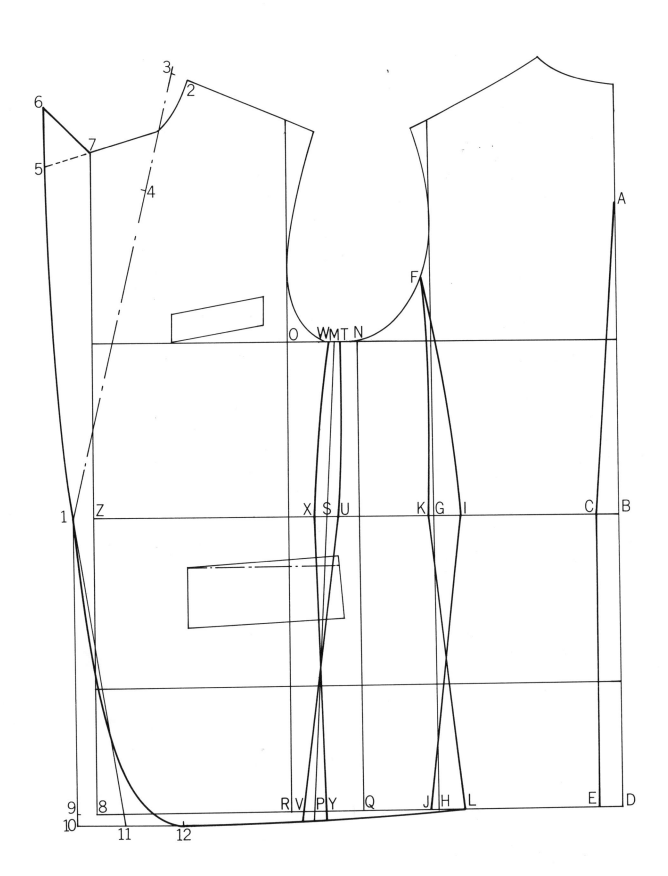

TWO BUTTON CONTINENTAL JACKET

Outline your jacket sloper with jacket length.

Back Panel
A = 1/2 neck to chestline.
B to C = 1".
C to D = 1".
E to F = 1".
Connect A to D and D to F with a straight line to finish center back.
G = 3" above chestline.
H = 1" above waistline.
H to J = 1/2".
Connect G to J with hip curve ruler.
Connect J to I with straight line to finish back panel.

Front Panel
H to K = 1/2".
Connect G to K with hip curve ruler.
Connect K to I with straight line.
L = 1/3 M to N.
Connect L to O as guideline.
P = 1" above waistline.
L to Q = 1/4".
P to R = 1/2".
P to S = 4 3/4".
Connect Q to R with hip curve ruler.
Connect R to S with hip curve ruler.
L to T = 1/4".
P to U = 1/2".
Connect T to U with hip curve ruler.
Connect U to S with straight line to finish dart.
V to W = 3/4" for extension.
W to X = 2".
Y = shoulder at neck.
Y to Z = collar stand.
Extend neckline and square off lapel width 1 to 2 according to design.
Connect 2 to X with hip curve ruler using a deeper curve toward 2.
3 to 4 = 3/4"
4 to 5 = 1/2".
5 to 6 = 1 1/4".
Connect W to 6 with straight line as a guide.
Connect W to 7 according to design.
Connect 7 to I with hip curve ruler.
8 = 1/2 9 to N.
10 = 1" above waistline.
10 to 11 = 3 1/4".
Connect 8 to 11 with straight line.
10 to 12 = 1/4".
Connect 8 to 12 with straight line.
Connect 12 to 11 with straight line to finish front panel.

Pocket, see page 132-134.
Collar, see page 188.
Buttonhole, see page 130.

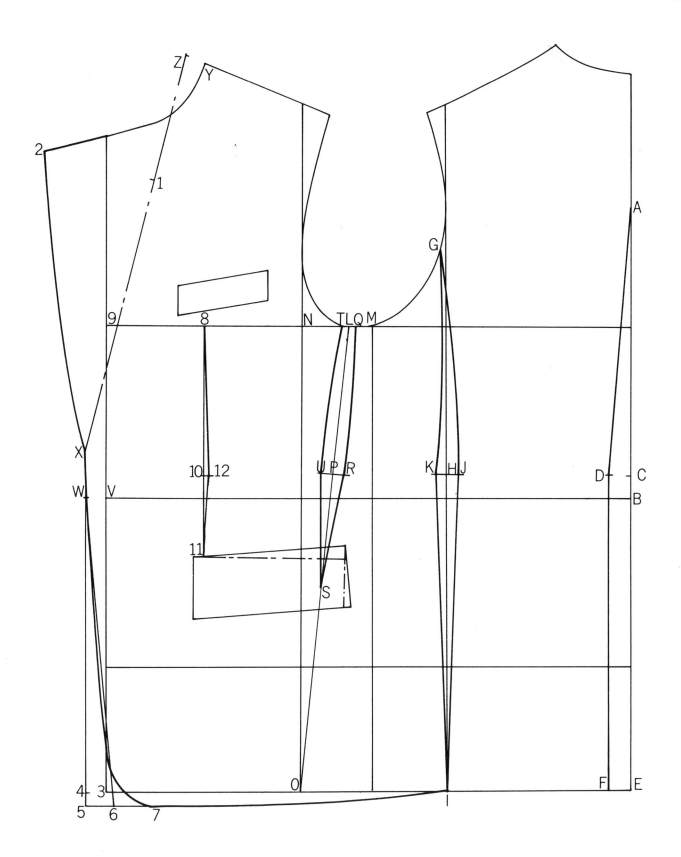

THREE BUTTON SINGLE BREASTED ITALIAN CUT JACKET

Outline your sloper with jacket length.

Back Panel
A = 1/2 neck to chest.
B to C = 1".
E to D = 1".
Connect A to C to E with straight line to finish center back.
F = 3" above chest line.
G to I = 1 1/4"
H to J = 1/2".
Connect F to I with hip curve ruler.
Connect I to J with straight line to finish back panel.

Front Panel
G to K = 1/4".
Connect F to K with shallow curve.
Connect K to J with straight line.
L = 1/3 M to N.
O = front side guideline at hem.
Connect L to O as guideline.
P is at waist on guideline.
L to Q = 1/4".
L to R = 1/4".
P to S = 1/2".
P to T = 1/2".
P to U = 4".
Connect Q to S with hip curve ruler.
Connect S to U with straight line.
Connect R to T with same curve as Q to S.
Connect T to U to finish side darts.
V = center front at waist.
V to W = 3/4" for extension.
V to X = 4".
X to Y = 3/4" for extension.
Connect Y to W and extend to hemline.
Z = shoulder neck point.
Z to 1 = collar stand.
Connect Y to 1 to establish roll line.
Extend neckline toward 2.
2 to 14 = width of lapel.
Connect 2 to Y with hip curve ruler, using deeper curve toward Y
    to finish lapel.
3 = center front at hem.
3 to 4 = 3/4".
4 to 5 = 1/2".
6 = 1/3 3 to O.
Connect W to 6 according to design.
Connect 6 to J with shallow curve.

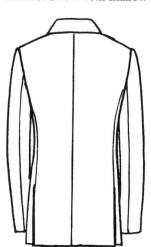

Front Dart
7 = 1/2 V to 8.
7 to 9 = 1/2".
Square down from 7 to 10.
Square down from 9 to 11.
10 to 11 = 1/2".
12 = 1/2 7 to 9.
Square up from 12 to chest 13.
Connect 7 to 13 and 9 to 13 to
    finish front dart.

Pocket, see pages 132–134.
Collar, see page 188.
Buttonhole, see page 130.

93

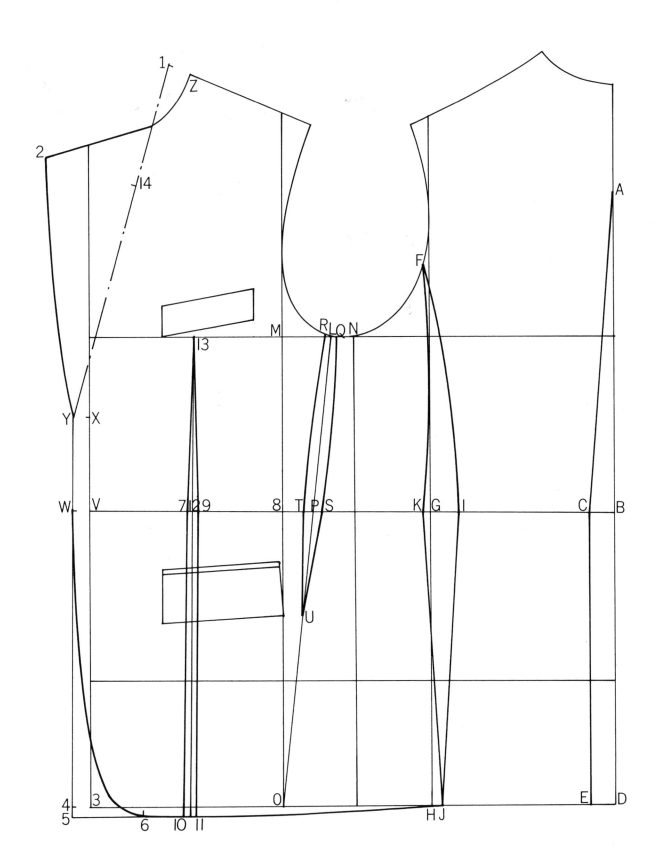

DIAGRAM—Three Button Single Breasted Italian Cut Jacket

TWO BUTTON DOUBLE BREASTED CONTINENTAL JACKET

Outline your sloper with jacket length.

Back Panel
A = 1/2 neck to chest.
B to C = 1".
D to E = 1".
Connect A to C to E with straight line to finish center back.
F = 3" above chest line.
G to I = 7/8".
H = hem.
Connect F to I with hip curve ruler.
Connect I to H with straight line to finish back panel.

Side Panel
G to J = 7/8".
H to K = 1".
Connect L to O with hip curve ruler (shallow section).
Connect J to K with straight line.
L = 1 1/2" above chest line.
M to O = 1/2".
N to P = 1/2".
Connect L to O with hip curve ruler.
Connect O to P with straight line to finish side panel.

Front Panel
L to Q = 3/8".
M to R = 1/2".
N to S = 1/2".
Connect Q to R with hip curve ruler.
Connect R to S with straight line.
T = center front at waist line.
T to U = 2 1/2" for extension.
V = shoulder at neck point.
V to W = collar stand.
Connect U to W to establish roll line.
Extend neckline to X.
Square off Y to X for width of lapel.
X to Z = 3".
X to 1 = 2 1/2".
Connect Z to U with hip curve ruler using deeper curve
    toward U.
Connect Z to 1 with straight line to finish lapel.
2 = center front at hem.
2 to 3 = 2 1/2" for extension.
3 to 4 = 1/2".
5 = 1/2 2 to P.
Connect U to 4 with straight line.
Square off from 4 to 5.
Connect 5 to K with hip curve ruler
    to finish front panel.

Front Dart
6 = 1/2 T to M.
Square up 6 to 7.
Square down 6 to 8.
6 to 9 = 1/4".
Connect 7 to 9 to 8 with straight
    line to finish front dart.

Pocket, see pages 132–134.
Collar, see page 188.
Buttonhole, see page 130.

DIAGRAM—Two Button Double Breasted Continental Jacket

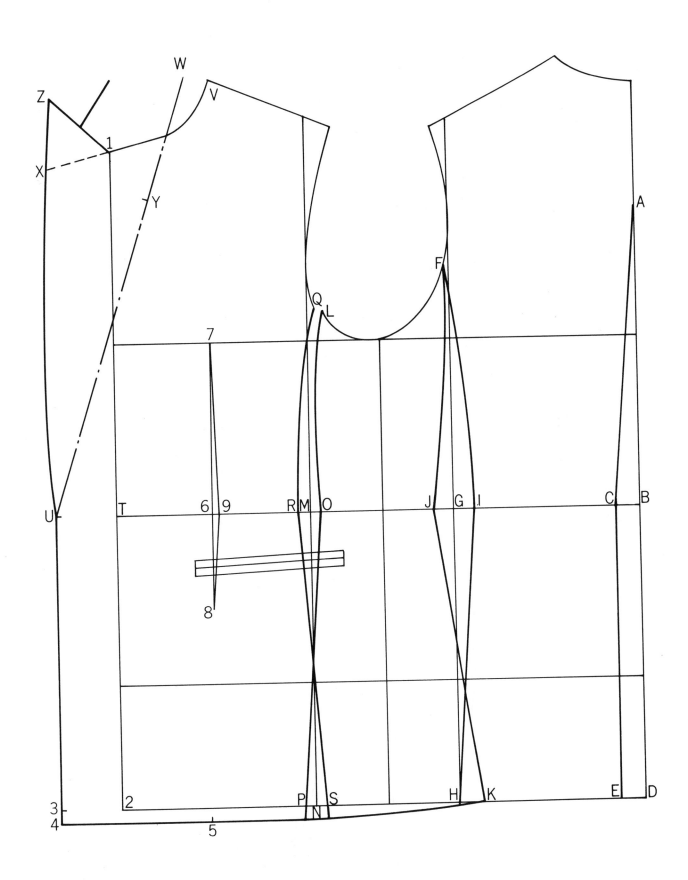

DOUBLE BREASTED CONTINENTAL JACKET

Outline your sloper with jacket length.

Back Panel
A = 1/2 neck to chest.
B to C = 1".
E to D = 3/4".
Connect A to C to E to finish center back.
F = 2 1/2" above chest.
G to I = 1 1/4".
H to J = 1/4".
Connect F to I with hip curve ruler.
Connect I to J with straight line to finish back panel.

Back Side Panel
G to K = 1/4".
H to L = 1 1/4".
Connect F to K with hip curve ruler.
Connect K to L with straight line.
M to N to O = side guideline.
N = 1" above waistline.
N to P = 1/4".
O to Q = 3/4".
Connect M to P with hip curve ruler.
Connect P to Q with straight line to finish back side panel.

Front Side Panel
M to R = 1/2".
N to S = 3/4".
O to T = 1/4".
Connect R to S with hip curve ruler.
Connect S to T with straight line.
U = 3" above chest line.
V to W = 1 1/2".
V to X = 3/4".
Y to Z = 1".
Connect U to X with hip curve ruler.
Connect X to Z with straight line to finish front side panel.

Front Panel
Connect U to V with hip curve ruler.
Connect V to Z with straight line.
1 = center front at waist.
1 to 2 = 1 1/2".
2 to 3 = 2 1/2" for extension.
4 = shoulder at neck point.
4 to 5 = collar stand.
Connect 3 to 5 to establish roll line.
Extend neckline to 6.
Square off from 7 to 6 for width of lapel.
6 to 8 = 3".
Connect 8 to 3 with hip curve ruler, using deeper curve
     toward 3.

9 = neck point.
Connect 8 to 9 to finish lapel.
10 = center front at hem.
10 to 11 = 2 1/2".
11 to 12 = 1/2".
Connect 3 to 12.
13 = 1/2 10 to Y.
Connect 13 to L with shallow curve
     to finish jacket.

Pocket, see pages 132–134.
Collar, see page 188.
Buttonhole, see page 130.

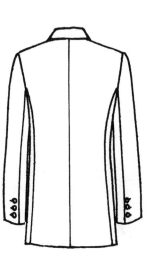

DIAGRAM–Double Breasted Continental Jacket

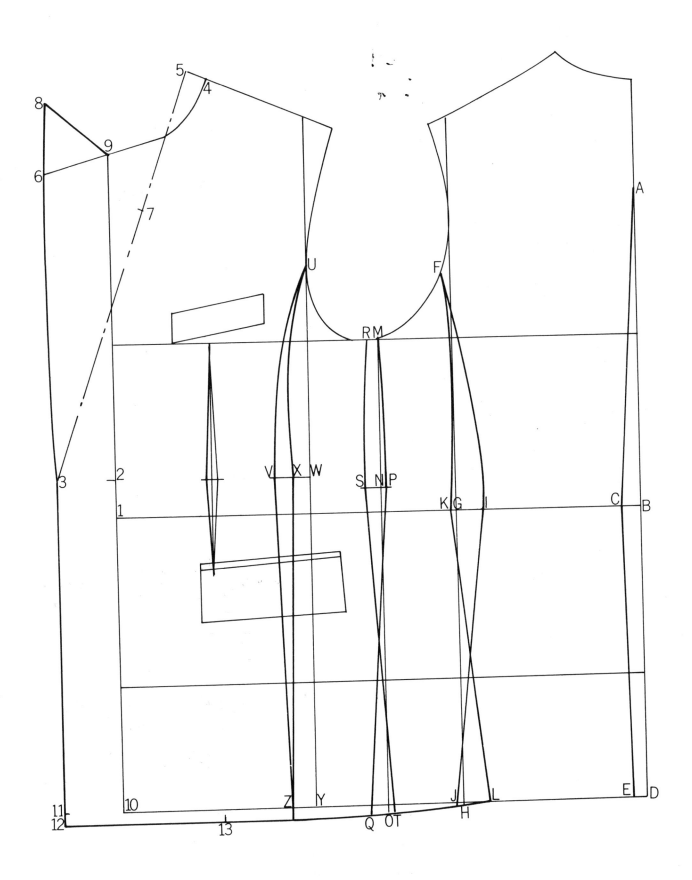

ITALIAN CUT JACKET

Outline your sloper with jacket length.

Back Panel
A = 1/2 neck to chest.
B to C = 3/4".
D to E = 3/4".
Connect A to C to E to finish center back.
F = 2 3/4" above chest line.
G to I = 1 1/4".
H to J = 1/2".
Connect F to I with hip curve ruler.
Connect I to J with straight line to finish back panel.

Side Panel
G to K = 1/4".
J to L = 1".
Connect F to K with hip curve ruler.
M = 1/2 N to O.
P to R = 1".
Connect M to R with hip curve ruler.
Connect R to Q with straight line to finish side panel.

Front
M to S = 1/2".
Q to T = 1".
Connect S to P with hip curve ruler.
Connect P to T with straight line.
U = waistline at center front.
U to V = 2 1/2".
V to X = 3/4".
Y = shoulder at neck.
Y to Z = collar stand.
Connect X to Z to finish roll line.
1 = roll line at neck.
Extend neckline toward 2.
Line between 1 and 2 is straight.
Square off from 3 to 2 for lapel width.
2 to 4 = 3".
5 = 1/2 1 to 2 to finish lapel.
6 = center front at hem.
6 to 7 = 3/4".
7 to 8 = 1/2".
Connect X to 8.
9 = 1/2 6 to Q.
Square off from 8 to 9.
8 to 10 = 1".
11 is at waist.
Connect 10 to 11 as guideline.
Connect 11 to 9 according to design.

Front Dart
12 = 1/2 13 to O.
Square down from 12 to 9
9 to 14 = 1".
Connect 14 to 12.
14 to 15 = 1/4".
14 to 16 = 1/4".
17 is at waist.
17 to 18 = 1/4".
17 to 19 = 1/4".
Connect 12 to 18 to 15.
Connect 12 to 19 to 16 to finish
front dart.

Neck Dart
a to 1 = 1".
a to b = 3/8".
a to c = 3".
Connect b to c to finish dart.

Pocket, see pages 132-134.
Collar, see page 188.
Buttonhole, see page 130.

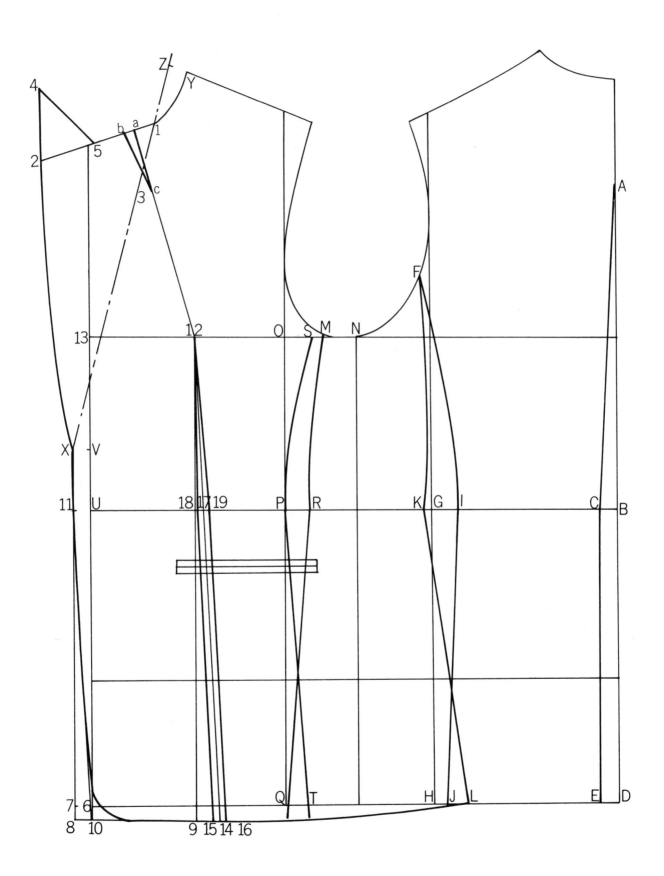

DRAPED DOUBLE BREASTED JACKET

Outline your sloper with jacket length.

Back Panel
A = 1/2 neck to chest.
B = 2" above waistline.
B to C = 1".
D to E = 1".
F = 4 1/2" above chest.
G = 1/4 B to H.
Square down from G to I.
I to J = 1/2".
G to K = 1".
Connect F to G with hip curve ruler.
Connect G to J with straight line.

Back Side Panel
Connect F to K with hip curve ruler.
Connect K to J with straight line.
L to M to N = side seam guideline.
L to O = 1/4".
M to P = 1/2".
N to Q = 1/2".
Connect O to P with hip curve ruler.
Connect P to Q with straight line to finish back side panel.

Front Side Panel
L to R = 1/4".
M to S = 1/2".
N to T = 1/2".
Connect R to S with same curve as O to P.
Connect S to T with straight line.
U = 1 1/2" above chest.
V to W = 1 1/4".
X to V = 1/2".
Y = hem at front side seam guideline.
Y to Z = 1 1/4".
Connect U to X with hip curve ruler.
Connect X to Z with straight line to finish front side panel.

Front Panel
Z to 1 = 1/2".
Connect U to V with hip curve ruler.
Connect V to 1 with straight line.
2 = waist at center front.
2 to 3 = 2".
3 to 4 = 2 1/2".
5 = shoulder at neck point.
5 to 6 = collar stand.
Extend neckline to 7.
Square off from 8 to 7 for width of lapel.
Connect 7 to 4 with hip curve ruler, with deeper curve toward 4.
9 = center front at hem.

9 to 10 = 2 1/2".
10 to 11 = 1/2".
Connect 4 to 11.
12 = 1/2 9 to Y.
Square off from 11 to 12
Connect 12 to J with shallow curve
   to finish jacket.

Pocket, see pages 132-134.
Collar, see page 188.
Buttonhole, see page 130.

DIAGRAM—Draped Double Breasted Jacket

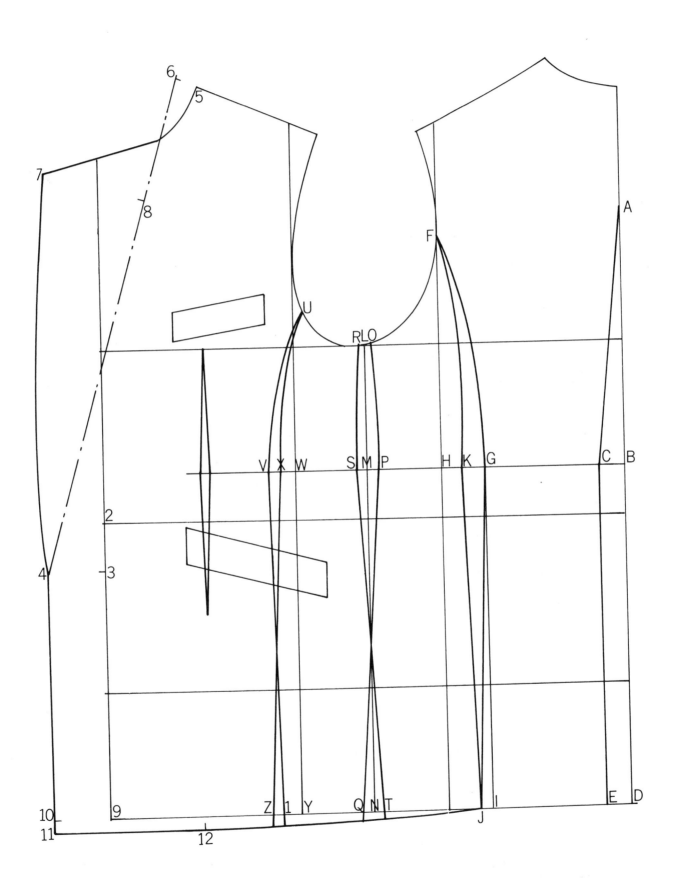

IVY LEAGUE JACKET

Drafting the Ivy League Jacket is similar to the basic blazer jacket with the exception of the lapel width, which is extremely narrow.

See Blazer Jacket Diagram

NOTES

BASIC JACKET DRAFTING PROCEDURE

Step 1

Step 2

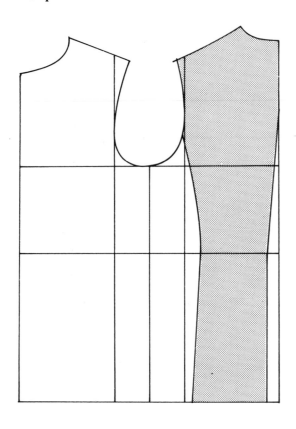

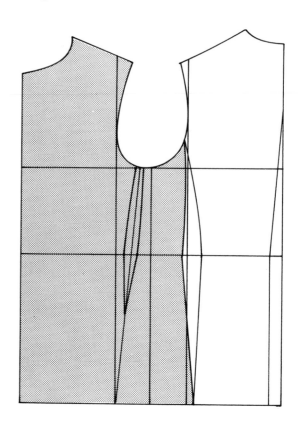

Step 3

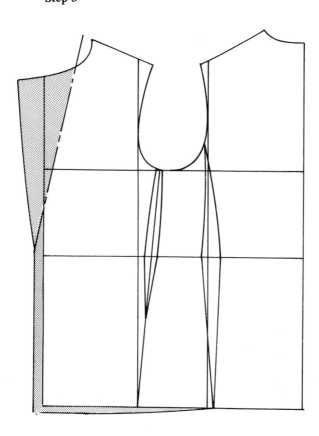

FITTED JACKET DRAFTING PROCEDURE

Step 1

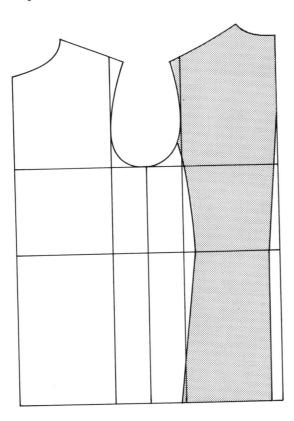

Step 2

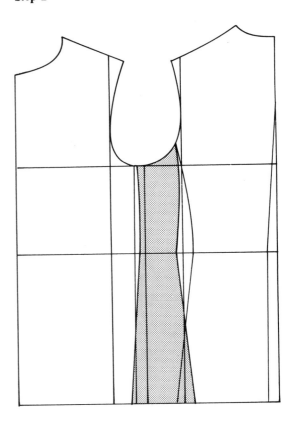

Step 3

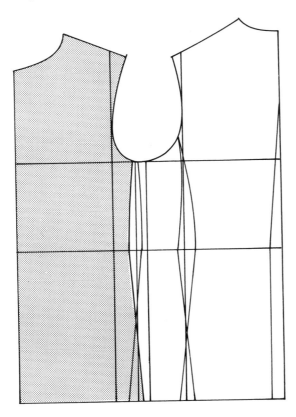

Step 4

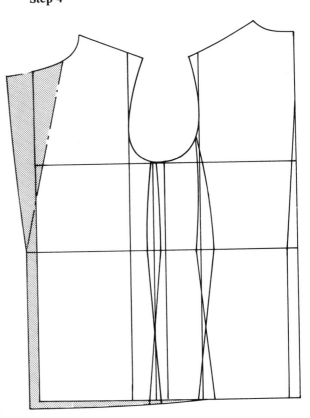

SHOULDER TORSO CUT JACKET

Outline your sloper with jacket length.

Back Panel
A = 1/2 B to C.
D = 1/2 E to F.
Square down from D to G.
G to H = 3/4".
D to I = 1 1/4".
Connect A to D with hip curve ruler.
Connect D to H with straight line to finish back panel.

Back Side Panel
Connect A to I with hip curve ruler.
Connect I to H with straight line.
J to K to L = side seam guideline.
J to M = 1/4".
K to N = 1/2".
Connect M to N with hip curve ruler.
Connect N to L with straight line to finish back side panel.

Front Side Panel
J to O = 1/4".
K to P = 1/2".
Connect O to P with hip curve ruler.
Connect P to L with straight line.
Q = 1/2 R to S.
T = 1/2 U to V.
Square down T to W.
W to X = 3/4".
T to Y = 3/4".
Connect Q to Y with curved line according to design line.
Connect Y to X with straight line to finish front side panel.

Front Panel
Connect Q to T according to design.
Connect T to X with straight line.
1 = center front at chest line.
1 to 2 = 3/4".
3 is at neck point.
3 to 4 = 1/2".
4 to 5 = 3/4".
Connect 1 to 4 with shallow curve.
Connect 5 to 2 with the same curve as 1 to 4.
6 = center front at hem.
6 to 7 = 3/4".
7 to 8 = 1/2".
Square off 8 to X
Connect X to H with shallow curve to finish jacket.

Pocket
T to a = 2 1/4".
T to b = 7 1/2".
b to c = 2 1/4".
Connect T to a to c to b according to design.

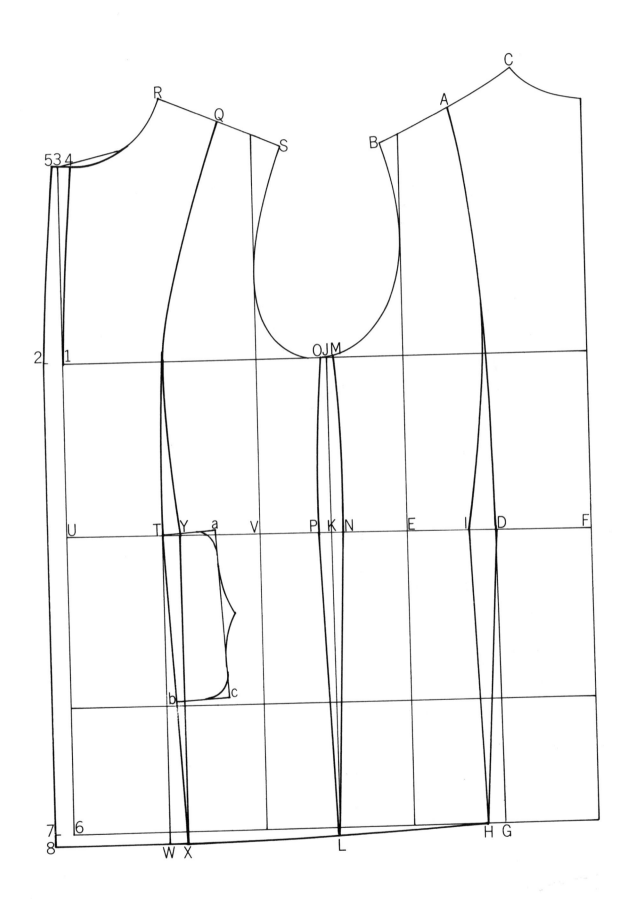

NECKLINE TORSO CUT JACKET

Outline your sloper with jacket length.

Back Panel
A = 1/2 neck to chest.
C to B = 1".
D to E = 3/4".
F = 1 1/2" above chest line.
G to H = 1".
I to J = 1".
Connect F to H with curved line.
Connect H to J with straight line to finish back
   panel.

Back Side Panel
Connect F to G with hip curve ruler.
Connect G to J with straight line.
K to L to M = side seam guideline.
K to N = 1/4".
L to O = 1/2".
M to P = 1/2".
Connect N to O with hip curve ruler.
Connect O to P with straight line to finish side
   panel.

Front Side Panel
K to Q = 1/4".
L to R = 1/2".
M to S = 1/2".
Connect Q to R with hip curve ruler.
Connect R to S with straight line.
T = neck point at center front.
U = 1/3 T to V.
U to X = 1/2".
Y = 1/2 Z to 1.
Square down from Y to 2.
2 to 3 = 3/4".
Connect Y to 3 for front seam.
4 = new seamline at waist.
4 to 5 = 1/2".
Connect X to Y with hip curve ruler, using deeper
   curve toward Y.
Connect Y to 5 to 3 to finish side panel.

Front Panel
Connect U to Y with hip curve ruler, according
   to design.
Connect Y to 3 with straight line to finish front
   design line.
T to 6 = 3/4" for extension.
7 = center front at hem.
            7 to 8 = 3/4".
            8 to 9 = 1/2".
            Connect 6 to 9.
            Square off from 9 to 3.
            Connect 3 to J with shallow curve
               to finish jacket.

109

DIAGRAM—Neckline Torso Cut Jacket

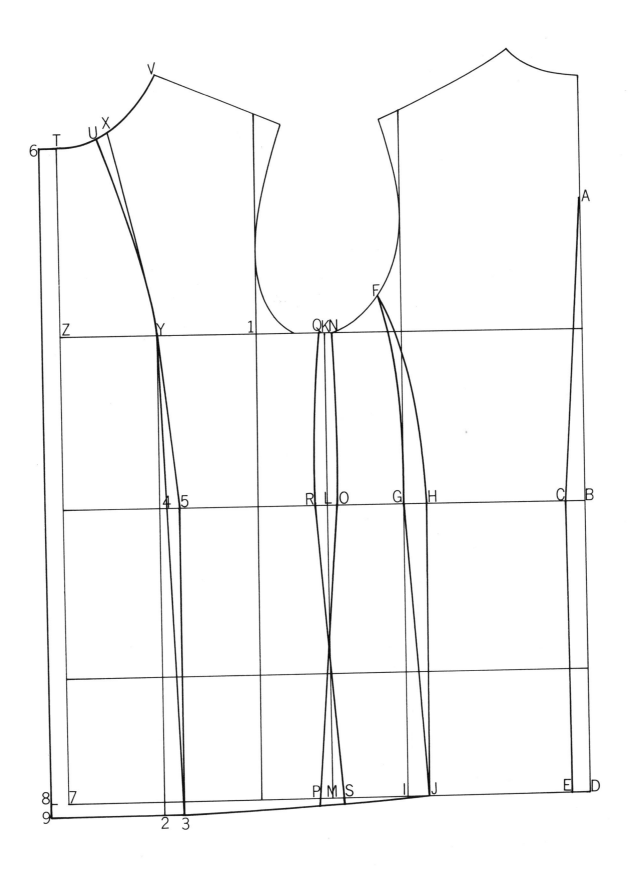

CENTER FRONT TORSO CUT JACKET

Outline your sloper with jacket length.

Back Panel
A = 1/2 neck to chest.
B to C = 1".
D to E = 3/4".
Connect A to C to E to finish center back.
F = 2" above chest line.
G to I = 1".
H to J = 1/2".
Connect F to I with hip curve ruler
Connect I to J with straight line to finish back panel.

Back Side Panel
Connect F to G with hip curve ruler.
Connect G to J with straight line
K to L to M = side seam guideline.
K to N = 1/4".
L to O = 1/2".
M to P = 1/2".
Connect N to O with hip curve ruler.
Connect O to P with straight line to finish back side
    panel.

Front Side Panel
K to Q = 1/4".
L to R = 1/2".
M to S = 1/2".
Connect Q to R with hip curve ruler.
Connect R to S with straight line.
T = neck point.
T to U = 1/2".
V = center front at chest line.
V to W = 3/4" for extension.
Square off from U to X 3/4" for extension.
Y = 1/3 X to W.
Z = 1/2 V to 1.
2 = located on lines squared from Y and Z.
Square down Z to 3.
4 = 1/2 2 to Z.
3 to 5 = 1/2".
Connect 4 to 5 with straight line.
6 to 7 = 3/8".
Connect Y to 4 according to design.
Connect 4 to 7 to 5 with straight line to finish
    front side panel.

Front Panel
Connect 4 to 5
8 to 9 = 3/4" for extension.
9 to 10 = 1/2".
Connect X to W to 10 with straight line.
Square off from 10 to 5.
Connect 5 to J with hip curve ruler to finish jacket.

DIAGRAM–Center Front Torso Cut Jacket

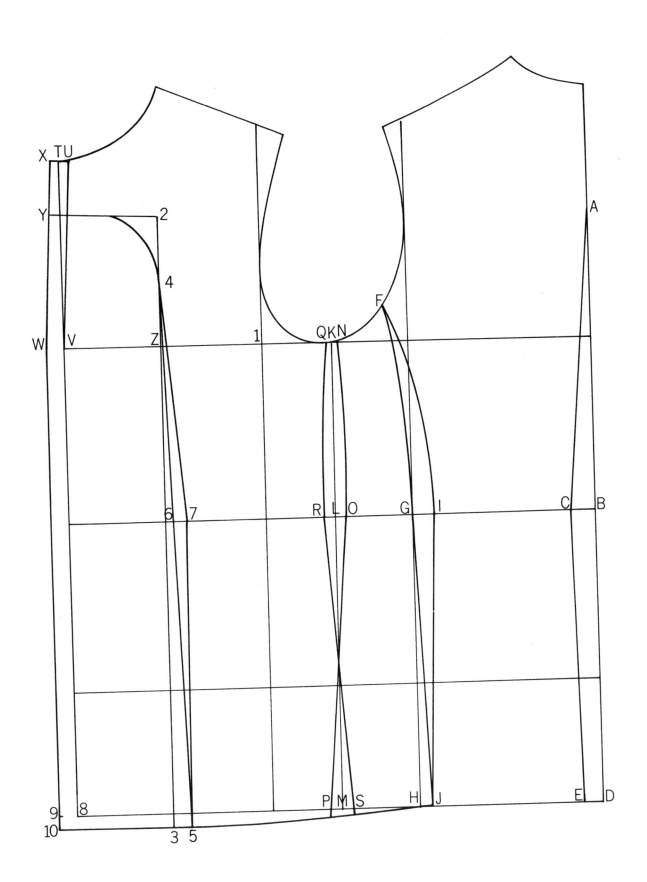

ARMHOLE TORSO CUT JACKET

Outline your sloper with jacket length.

Back Panel
C = 1/2 A to B.
E = 1/2 D to F.
Square down from E to G.
H to G = 3/4".
Connect C to E with curved line according to design.
Connect E to H with straight line to finish back panel.

Back Side Panel
E to I = 1 1/2".
Connect C to I with curved line.
Connect I to H with straight line.
J to K to L = side seam guideline.
J to M = 1/4".
K to N = 1/2".
Connect M to N with hip curve ruler.
Connect N to L with straight line to finish back side panel.

Front Side Panel
J to O = 1/4".
K to P = 1/2".
Connect O to P with same curve as M to N.
Connect P to L with straight line.
Q = 1/2 R to S.
T = 1/2 U to V.
Square down from T to W.
W to X = 3/4".
T to Y = 3/4".
Connect Q to T with curved line according to design.
Connect T to X with straight line.
Connect Q to Y with curved line.
Connect Y to X with straight line.
Z = center front at chest line.
Z to 1 = 3/4".
2 = neck point.
2 to 3 = 3/8".
3 to 4 = 3/4".
Connect Z to 3 with shallow curve.
Connect 1 to 4 with same curve.

Square off from 3 to 4.
Blend in neckline.
5 = center front at hem.
6 to 5 = 3/4".
6 to 7 = 1/2".
Connect 1 to 7.
Square off from 7 to X.
Connect X to H with shallow curve to finish jacket.

Pocket, see pages 132-134.

113

DIAGRAM—Armhole Torso Cut Jacket

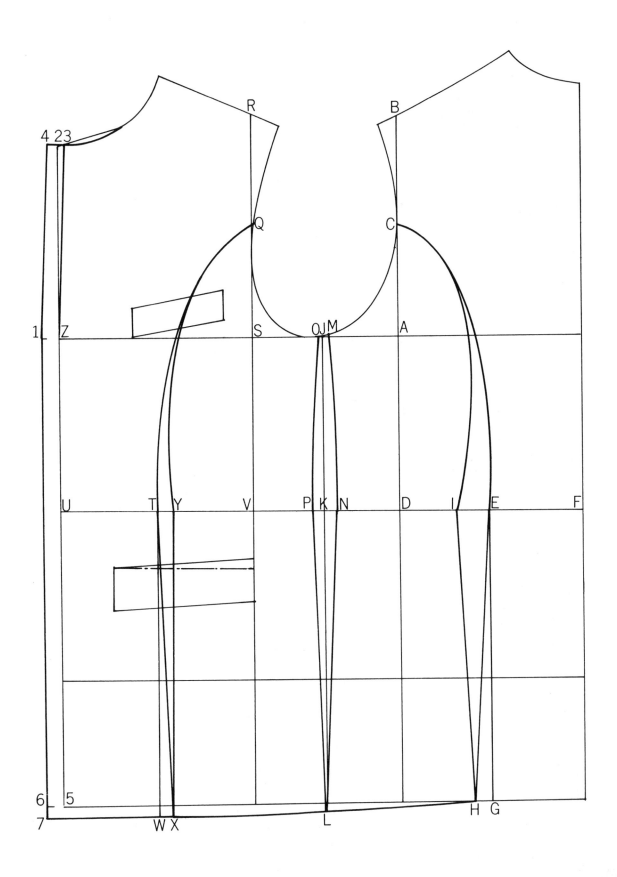

ARMHOLE TORSO CUT JACKET VARIATION

Outline your sloper with jacket length.

Back Panel

A = 1/2 neck to chest.
B to C = 3/4".
D to E = 3/4".
Connect A to C to E, to finish center back.
F = 4" above chest line.
G to I = 1".
H to J = 1/2".
Connect F to I with hip curve ruler.
Connect I to J with straight line to finish back panel.

Back Side Panel

Connect F to G with hip curve ruler.
Connect G to J with straight line.
K to L to M is side seam guideline.
K to N = 1/4".
L to O = 1/2".
M to P = 1/2".
Connect N to O with hip curve ruler.
Connect O to P with straight line to finish back side panel.

Side Panel

K to Q = 1/4".
L to R = 1/2".
M to S = 1/2".
Connect Q to R with same curve as N to O.
Connect R to S with straight line.
T = 1" above chest line.
U to V = 1/2".
W to X = 1-1/4".
Connect T to V with hip curve ruler.
Connect V to X with straight line to finish side panel.

Front Side Panel

V to Y = 1/2".
X to Z = 1/2".
Connect T to Y with hip curve ruler.
Connect Y to Z with straight line.
1 = 1/2 2 to 3.
4 = 1/2 5 to U.
Square down from 4 to 6.
4 to 7 = 1/2".
Connect 1 to 7 with curved line.
Connect 7 to 6 with straight line.

Front Panel

Connect 1 to 4 with curved line.

6 to 8 = 1/2".
Connect 4 to 8 with straight line.
5 to 9 = 2".
9 to 10 = 3/4".
11 = shoulder at neck point.
11 to 12 = collar stand.
Connect 10 to 12.
Extend neckline toward 13.
Square off 14 to 13 for lapel width.
Connect 13 to 10 with hip curve ruler,
   using deeper curve toward 10.
15 is center front at hem.
15 to 16 = 3/4".
16 to 17 = 1/2".
Square off from 17 to 8.
Connect 8 to J with shallow curve to
   finish jacket.

DIAGRAM–Armhole Torso Cut Jacket Variation

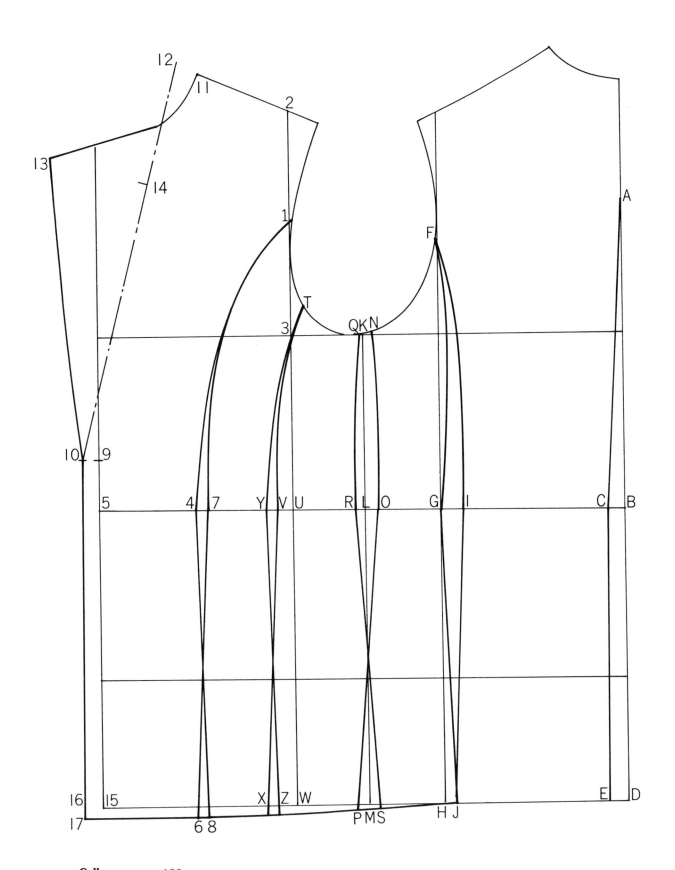

Collar, see page 188.
Buttonhole, see page 130.

FOUR BASIC TORSO CUT JACKETS

Shoulder Torso Cut Jacket

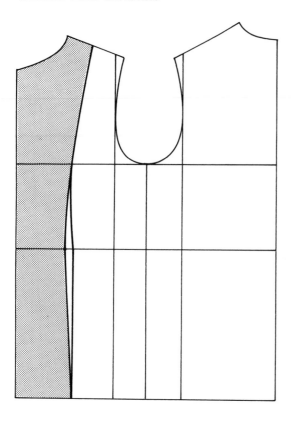

Armhole Torso Cut Jacket

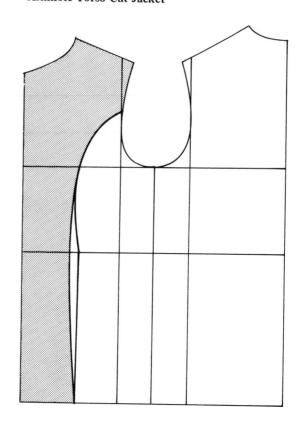

Center Front Torso Cut Jacket

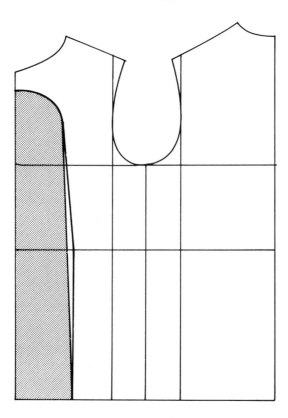

Neck Torso Cut Jacket

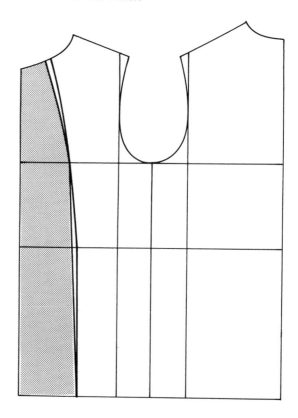

NOTES

DINNER JACKET

Outline your sloper with jacket length.

Back Panel
A = 1/2 neck to chest.
B to C = 1".
D to E = 1".
Connect A to C to E with straight line to finish center back.
F = 3" above chestline.
G to I = 3/4".
H to J = 1/4".
Connect F to I with hip curve ruler.
Connect I to J with straight line to finish back panel.

Side Panel
G to K = 1/4".
H to L = 3/4".
Connect F to K with hip curve ruler.
Connect K to L with straight line.
O = 1/3 M to N.
Square off O to P as guideline.
Q is on waistline.
O to R = 1/4".
Q to S = 1/2".
P to T = 5/8".
Connect R to S with hip curve ruler.
Connect S to T with straight line to finish side panel.

Front Panel
O to U = 1/4".
Q to V = 1/2".
P to W = 5/8".
Connect U to V with hip curve ruler.
Connect V to W with straight line.
X = center front on waistline.
X to Y = 1 1/2".
Y to Z = 3/4" for extension.
1 = 1/2" below sloper hemline.
Square off from Z to 1.
Square off from 1 to 2.
Connect Z to 2 according to design.
Connect 2 to L with hip curve ruler.

Shawl Collar
Z = break point.
3 = shoulder at neck.
3 to 4 = collar stand.
Connect Z to 4.
4 to 5 = back neck measurement.
5 to 6 = 1/2" shift.
6 to 7 = collar stand.
8 = deepest section of neck.
9 = shoulder at neck.
9 to 7 = back neck measurement.
Square off 7 to 10.
6 to 10 = 1 1/2" (Fall = stand + 3/8").
Square off 11 to 12, 3".
Connect 12 to Z according to design.
Square off 10 to 13.
Blend 13 to 12 to finish collar.

Darts
14 = 1/2 N to 15.
Square down 14 to 2.
2 to 16 = 1/2".
Connect 14 to 16.
17 to 18 = 1/2".
16 to 19 = 1/2".
Connect 14 to 18 to 19 to finish front dart.
Extend neckline to 12.

See **Pocket**, pages 132–134.

DIAGRAM—Dinner Jacket

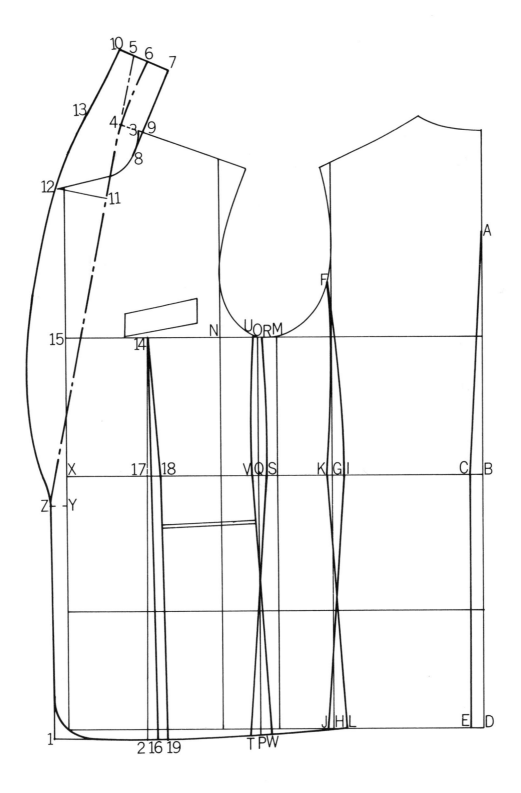

Note: Cut front facing and upper collar into one piece.

LINK FRONT EVENING JACKET

Outline your sloper with jacket length.

Back Panel

A = 1/2 neck to chest.
B to C = 1".
D to E = 3/4".
Connect A to C to E with straight line to finish center back.
F = 1/2 G to H.
I = 1/3 J to C.
I to K = 1-1/2".
L = 1/2 K to I.
Square down from L to M.
M to N = 3/4".
Connect F to I with hip curve ruler.
Connect I to N with straight line to finish back panel.

Back Side Panel

M to O = 3/4".
Connect F to K with hip curve ruler.
Connect K to O with straight line.
P to Q to R = side seam guideline.
P to S = 1/4".
Q to T = 3/4".
R to U = 1/2".
Connect S to T with hip curve ruler.
Connect T to U with straight line to finish back side panel.

Front Side Panel

P to V = 1/4".
Q to W = 3/4".
R to X = 1/2".
Connect V to W with curved line, same as S to T.
Connect W to X with straight line.
Y = 1/3 Z to 1.
2 = 1/3 3 to 4.
2 to 5 = 1".
6 = 1/2 2 to 5.
Square down from 6 to 7 as guideline.
7 to 8 = 1/2".
Connect Y to 5 with hip curve ruler.
Connect 5 to 8 with straight line to finish front side panel.

Front Panel

7 to 9 = 1/2".
Connect Y to 2 with hip curve ruler.
Connect 2 to 9 with straight line.
3 = center front on waistline.
3 to 10 = 1".
5 = center front on hemline.
5 to 6 = 1".
6 to 11 = 1/2".
Connect 10 to 11 with straight line for new center front.

12 = shoulder at neck point.
Connect 12 to 10 with straight line.
13 is on chest line.
13 to 14 = 1/4".
Connect 12 to 14 to 10 with hip curve ruler to finish new front design line.
Square off 11 to 9.
Connect 9 to O with shallow curve to finish jacket.

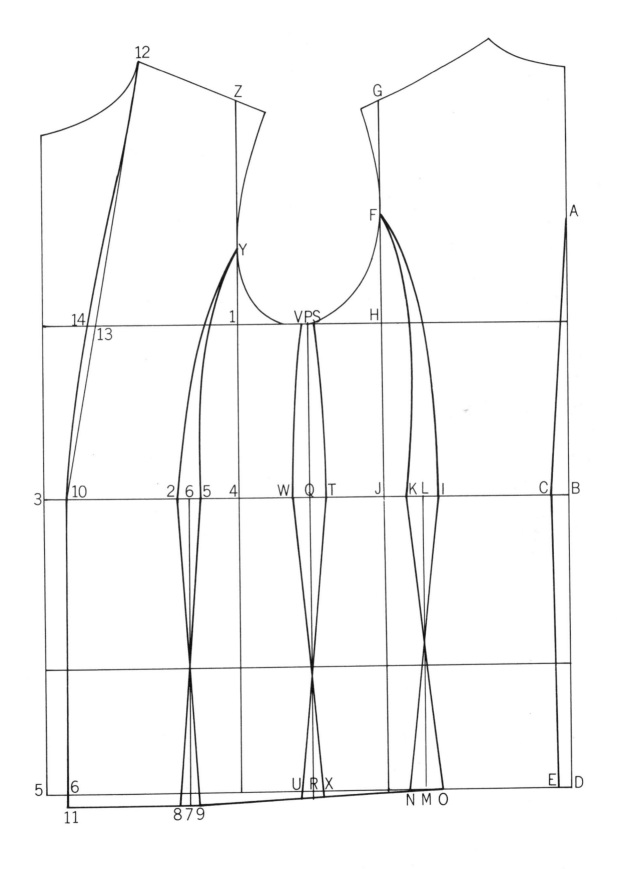

BASIC CAPE

Outline your jacket sloper.

Front Panel

DIAGRAM A

Extend chestline to B.
A to B = A to C.
D = shoulder point at armhole.
Connect D to B with straight line.

DIAGRAM B

E to F = cape length.
E to G, E to H, and E to I = E to F.
Connect F, G, H, and I with hip curve ruler to finish front
hemline.

DIAGRAM C

D to J = 6".
J to K = 1/2".

DIAGRAM D

Connect K to shoulder line with sleigh curve.
I to L = 1/2".
Connect K to L with straight line to finish front.

Back Panel
Use the same method for drafting the cape front.

DIAGRAM—Basic Cape

A

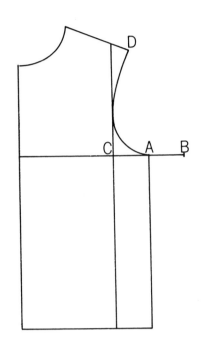

B

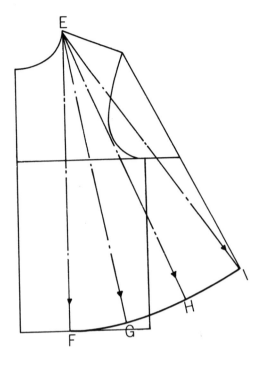

C

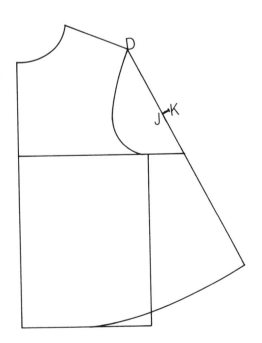

D

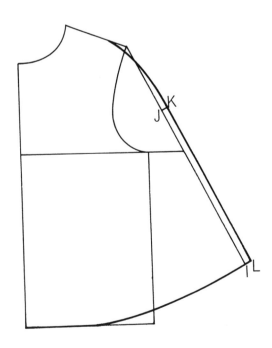

LONG FLARED CAPE

Use the method shown for drafting the basic cape.

The front tab is 2 1/2" wide, see diagram.

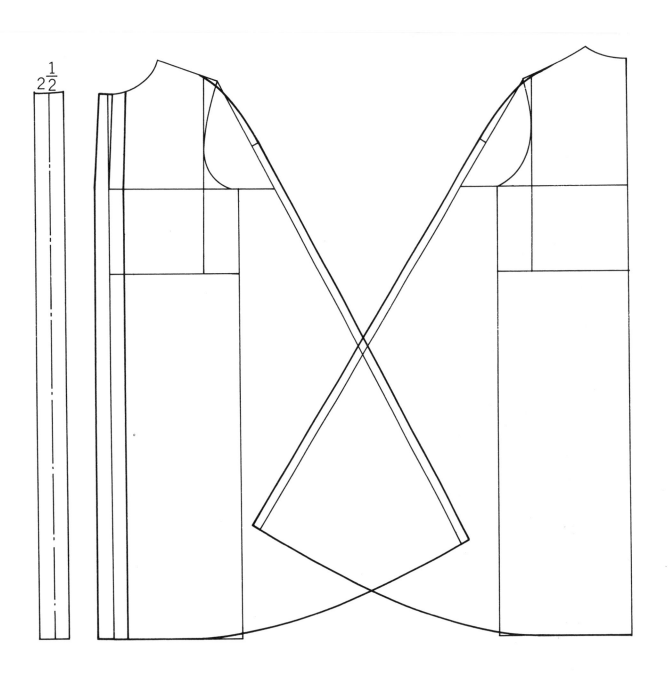

$2\frac{1}{2}$

TAILORED CAPE

Outline your basic sloper.

Front Panel
Extend chestline to B.
A to B = A to C.
D = armhole at shoulder.
Connect D to B with straight line as a guide.
D to E = 6".
E to F = 1/2".
Connect D to B with sleigh curve ruler, blending
    at point D.
Determine hemline according to basic cape instruc-
    tions on pages 122 and 123.

G = chestline at center front.
G to H = 1-1/2" for extension.
Square down from H to I.
J to K = A to G.
L = neckpoint.
L to M = 3/8".
Square off from M to N = 1-1/2" for extension.
Connect M to G with straight line.
Connect N to H with straight line to finish center
    front.

Back Panel
Use the same method for drafting the cape front,
    excluding the extension.

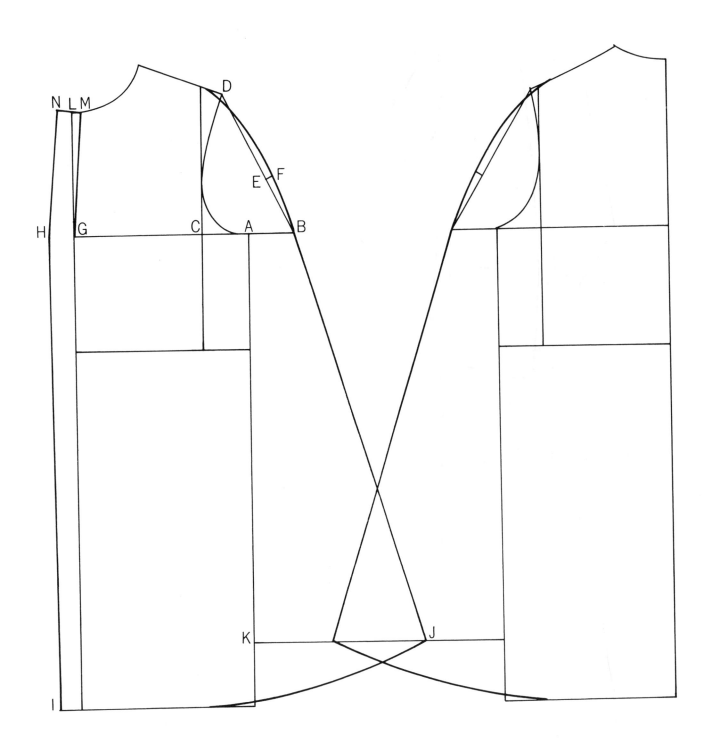

BUTTONHOLE DESIGN FOR CASUAL JACKET

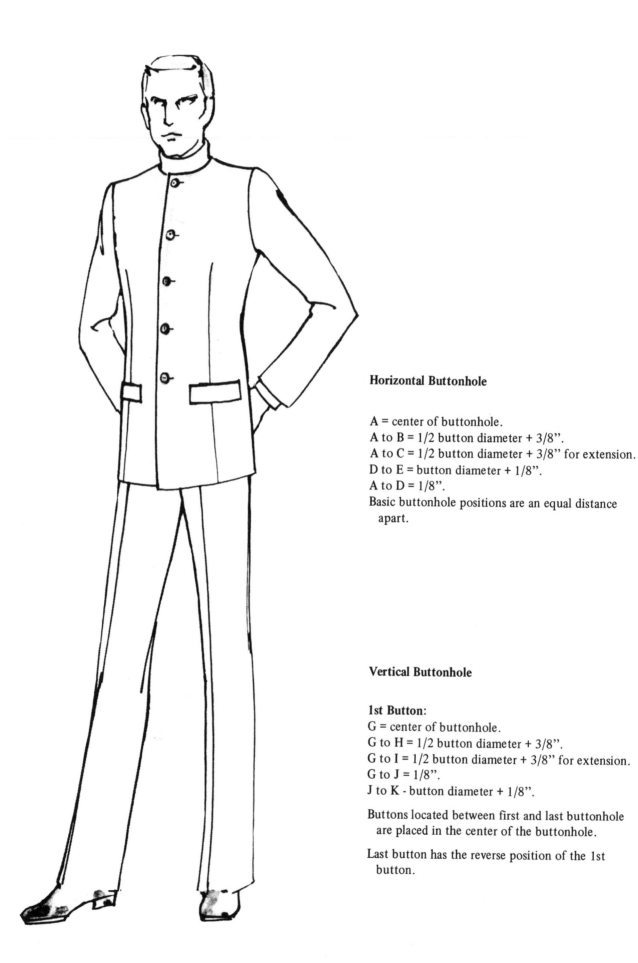

Horizontal Buttonhole

A = center of buttonhole.
A to B = 1/2 button diameter + 3/8".
A to C = 1/2 button diameter + 3/8" for extension.
D to E = button diameter + 1/8".
A to D = 1/8".
Basic buttonhole positions are an equal distance apart.

Vertical Buttonhole

1st Button:
G = center of buttonhole.
G to H = 1/2 button diameter + 3/8".
G to I = 1/2 button diameter + 3/8" for extension.
G to J = 1/8".
J to K - button diameter + 1/8".

Buttons located between first and last buttonhole are placed in the center of the buttonhole.

Last button has the reverse position of the 1st button.

DIAGRAM–Buttonhole Design for Casual Jacket

Horizontal

Vertical

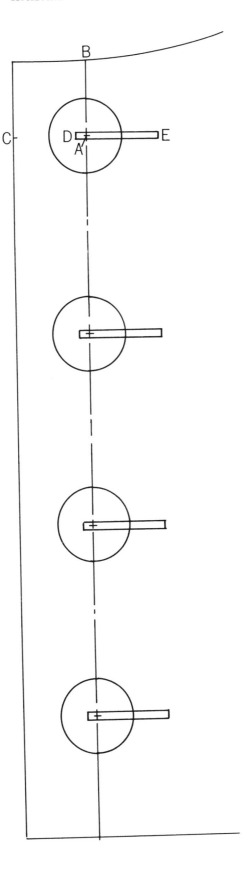

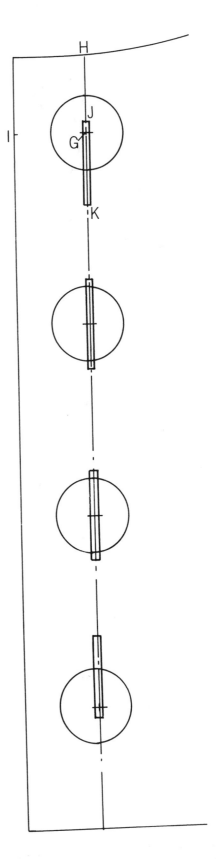

BUTTONHOLE DESIGN FOR TAILORED JACKET

Single-Breasted Jacket Buttonhole

A = center front on waistline.
A to B = 2".
C = Break point.
B to C = 1/2 buttonhole diameter + 3/8" for extension.
B to D = 1/8".
D to E = button diameter + 1/8".
A to F = 2" then repeat procedure.

Double-Breasted Jacket Buttonhole

A = center front.
B = the same as single-breasted jacket buttonhole.
A to C = A to B.

DIAGRAM—Buttonhole Design for Tailored Jacket

DIAGRAM—Single-Breasted Jacket Buttonhole

DIAGRAM—Double-Breasted Jacket Buttonhole

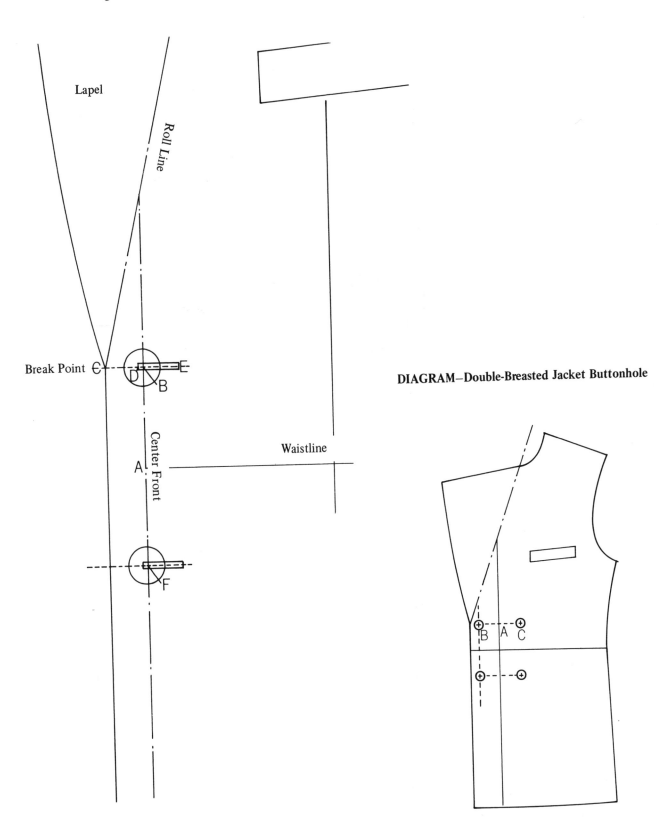

POCKETS

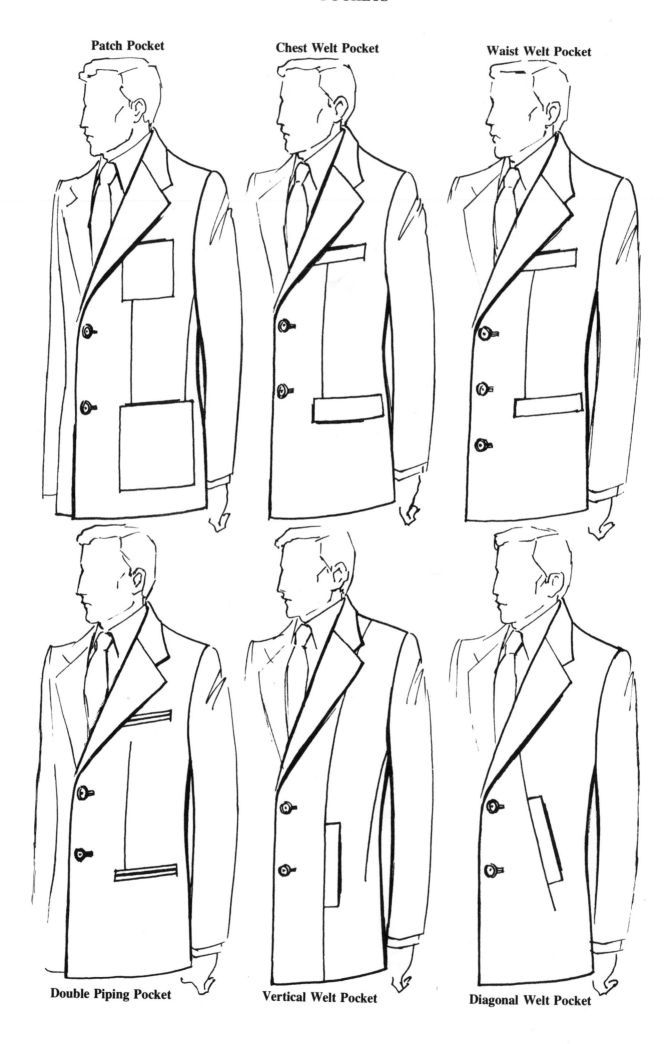

Patch Pocket

Chest Welt Pocket

Waist Welt Pocket

Double Piping Pocket

Vertical Welt Pocket

Diagonal Welt Pocket

POCKETS

Patch Pocket   **Chest Welt Pocket**

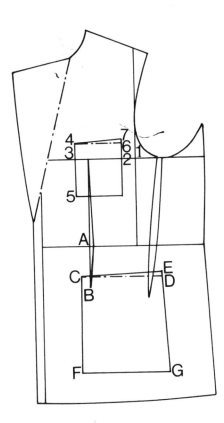 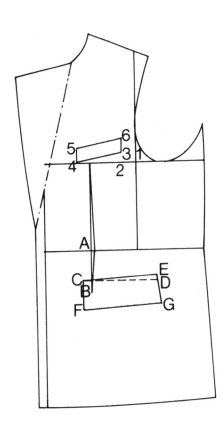

NOTE: The pockets shown on these pages are shown in minimum size. The size may be varied according to the design.

Waist Pocket

A to B = 2 1/2".
B to C = 3/4".
C to D = 7".
D to E = 3/8".
Connect C to E.
C to F = 8".
Square off from F to G.
Square off from E to G.
Connect C to F to G to E.

Chest Pocket

1 to 2 = 1 1/4".
2 to 3 = 4".
3 to 4 = 1 1/4".
4 to 5 = 4 1/2".
Connect 4 to 5.
2 to 6 = 1 1/4".
6 to 7 = 3/8".
Connect 4 to 7.
7 to 8 = 4 7/8".
5 to 8 = 4".
Connect 5 to 8 to 7.

Chest Welt Pocket

1 to 2 = 1 1/4".
2 to 3 = 3/4".
3 to 4 = 4".
4 to 5 = 1".
3 to 6 = 1".
Connect 4 to 5 to 6 to 3.

Flap Pocket

A to B = 2 1/2".
B to C = 3/4".
C to D = 6 1/2".
D to E = 3/8".
Connect C to E.
C to F = 2 1/2".
Square off E to G for 2 1/2".
Connect F to G to finish pocket.

POCKETS

Waist Welt Pocket   **Double Piping Pocket**

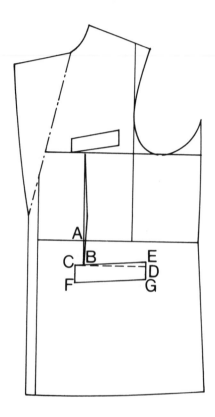 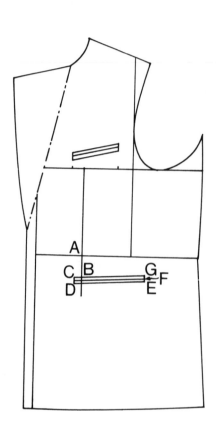

NOTE: The pockets shown on these pages are shown in minimum size. The size may be varied according to the design.

A to B = 2 1/2".
B to C = 3/4".
C to D = 6 1/2".
D to E = 3/8".
Connect C to E.
C to F is parallel to center front.
C to F = 1 1/2".
E to G = 1 1/2" parallel to center front.
Connect C to F to G to E to finish pocket.

Waist Pocket
A to B = 2 1/2".
B to C = 3/4".
C to D = 3/8".
D to E = 6 1/2".
E to F = 3/8".
F to G = 3/8".
Connect C to D, D to F, F to G, G to C, to finish pocket.
   Draw in middle opening line.

Chest Pocket
Angle, position and size of pocket will be the same as
   first three pockets.

POCKETS

Vertical Welt Pocket   **Diagonal Welt Pocket**

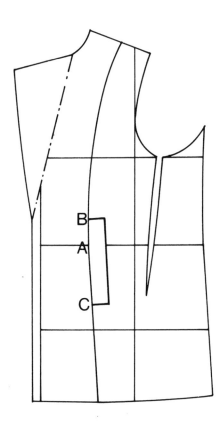

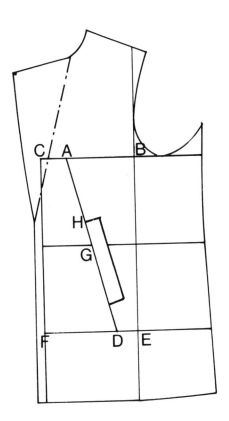

NOTE: The pockets shown on these pages are shown in minimum size. The size may be varied according to the design.

Design shoulder torso line. See **Shoulder Torso Line,** page 106.
A to B = 2".
B to C = 7".
Draft width of welt according to design.

A = 1/3 B to C.
D = 1/3 E to F.
Connect A to D.
G to H = 2".
H to I = 7".
Draft width of welt according to design.

BASIC SLEEVE SLOPER

Diagram 1

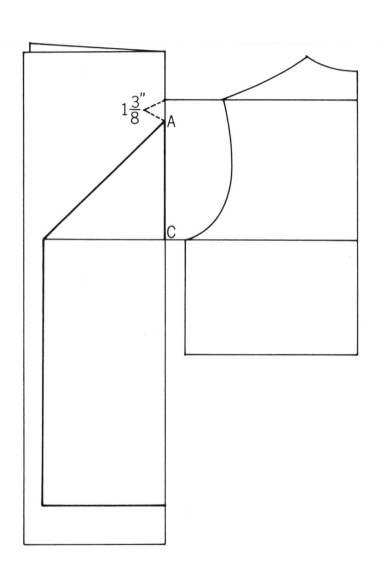

Diagram 2

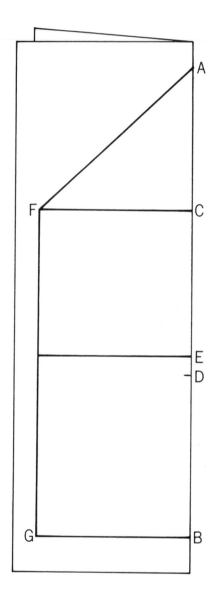

Prepare square of paper 32" X 32" and fold in half as in diagram.

Measurements needed:

Cap height.
Sleeve length. see page 6 to 7

In order to find cap height A to C, take armhole height from the Jacket Sloper, then take out 1-3/8".
(See diagram.)

A to B = sleeve length.
A to C = cap height.

For **Cap Height**, see pages 6–7.

D = 1/2 C to B.
D to E = 1".
Square off from C, E, and B toward left.
A to F = 1/2 armhole + 3/8".
Square down from F to G.

BASIC SLEEVE SLOPER

Diagram 3

Diagram 4

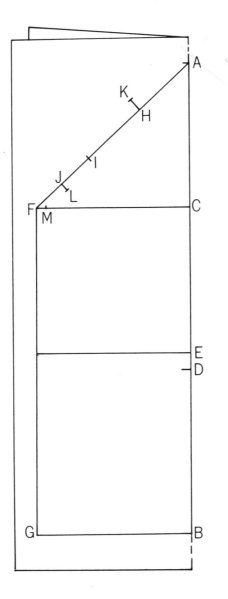

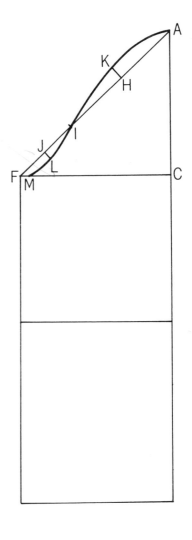

H = 1/3 A to F.
I = 1/3 A to F.
J = 1/2 I to F.
H to K = 3/4".
J to L = 3/8".
F to M = 1/2".

Connect A to K to I with sleigh curve ruler.
Reverse ruler to connect I to L to M.
Blend in at point M to finish back.

BASIC SLEEVE SLOPER

Diagram 5

Diagram 6

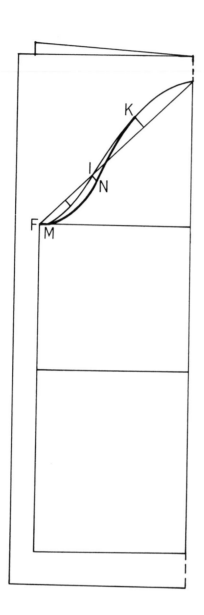

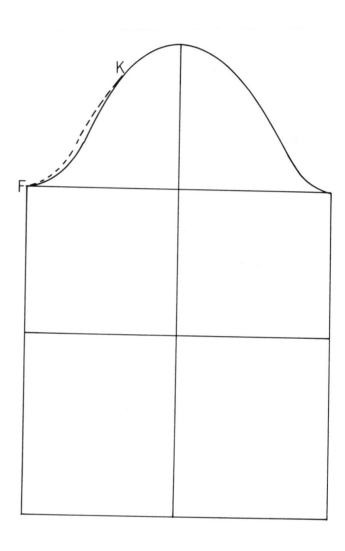

I to N = 3/8" for front sleeve cap.

Connect K to N with sleigh curve ruler.

Connect M to N with sleigh curve ruler and blend in to
 F to finish front.

Note: Front sleeve cap is deeper than back cap.

Trace sleeve cap, inseam and cuff.

Then open paper.

For left side of sleeve take off curve K to F for the
 front of sleeve.

BASIC SLEEVE SLOPER

Diagram 7

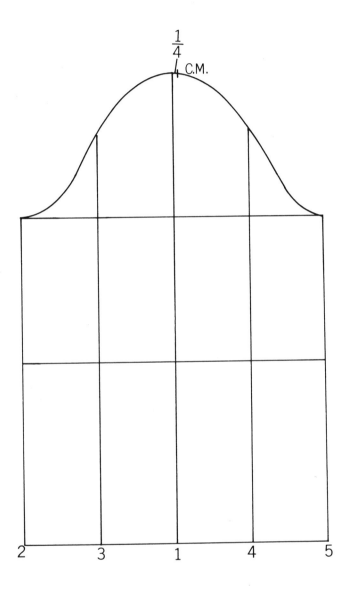

3 = 1/2 1 to 2.
4 = 1/2 1 to 5.
Square up from 3 and 4 to establish guideline.

Note: For additional underarm ease, see page 156—Diagram B,
for front and back sleeve.

ONE-PIECE SLEEVE

Outline sleeve sloper.

A to B = 5 1/2".
A to C = 5 1/2".
C to D = 3/8".
Connect E to D with hip curve ruler.
Connect F to B with hip curve ruler.
Connect A to D.
G to H = 2".
G to I = 2".
E to K = F to H.
J to D = I to B.
K to J = 3/8" longer than H to I for ease.

Note: The average cuff measurement is 11"–12". This may be changed according to your design.

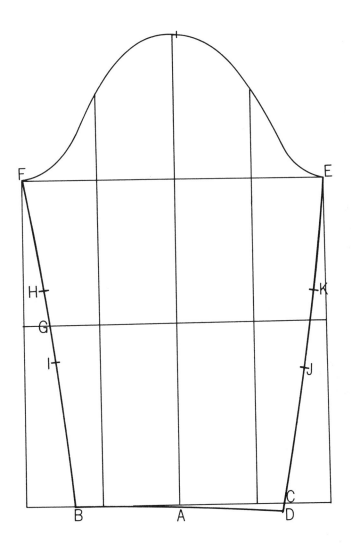

CUFFED SLEEVE

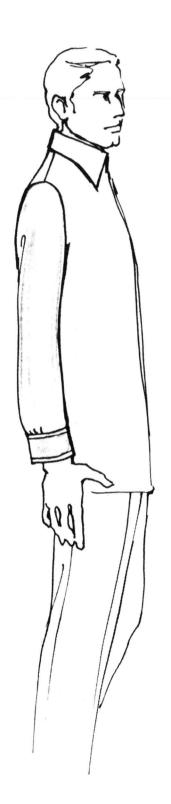

Outline sleeve sloper.

A to B = 4-1/4".
A to C = 4-1/4".
C to D = 3/8".
Connect E to B with straight line.
Connect F to D with straight line.
B to G = 2-1/2".
D to H = 2-1/2".
Remove B to G, G to H, H to D, and D to B for cuff.
I = 1/2 J to H.
I to K = 3" for opening.
J to L = 3/4".
L to M = 1/2" for pleat.
J to N = 1/2" for pleat.
N to O = 3/4".
O to P = 1/2" for pleat.

Cuff
R to S = length of cuff + 1" extension.
S to T = 2-1/2".
R to U = 1/2" for extension.
S to V = 1/2" for extension to finish cuff.

Note: The average cuff measurement is 9"- 11". This may be changed according to your design.

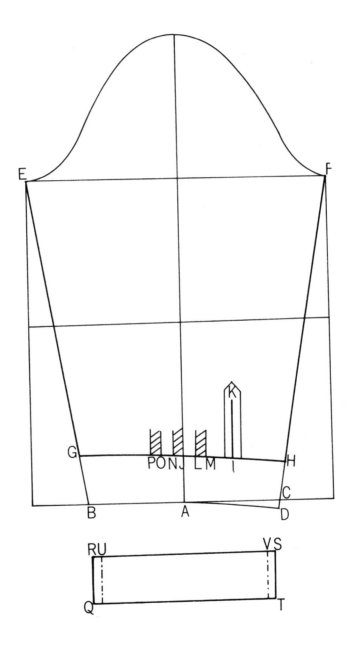

TWO PIECE SLEEVE

Under Sleeve   Upper Sleeve

TWO PIECE SLEEVE

Diagram A   **Diagram B**

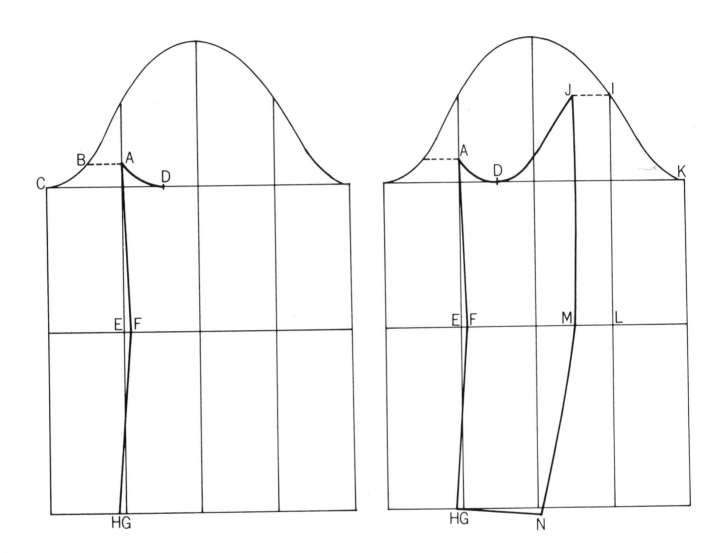

Under Sleeve

Outline sleeve sloper.

Two piece sleeve consists of upper sleeve and under sleeve.

On front guideline, square off from A to B for 2".
Transfer curve between B and C to A and D.
E to F = 3/8".
H to G = 3/8".
Connect A to F and F to H to finish inseam.

Square off top of back guideline I to J for 2".
Transfer curve between I and K to J and D.
L to M = I to J.
Square off from H to N.
H to N = 1/2 cuff minus 1" (circumference).
Connect J to M with shallowest part of hip curve ruler.
Connect M to N with shallowest part of hip curve ruler
    to finish under sleeve.

Note: The average cuff measurement is 11"–12". This may be
changed according to your design.

TWO PIECE SLEEVE

Diagram C   **Diagram D**

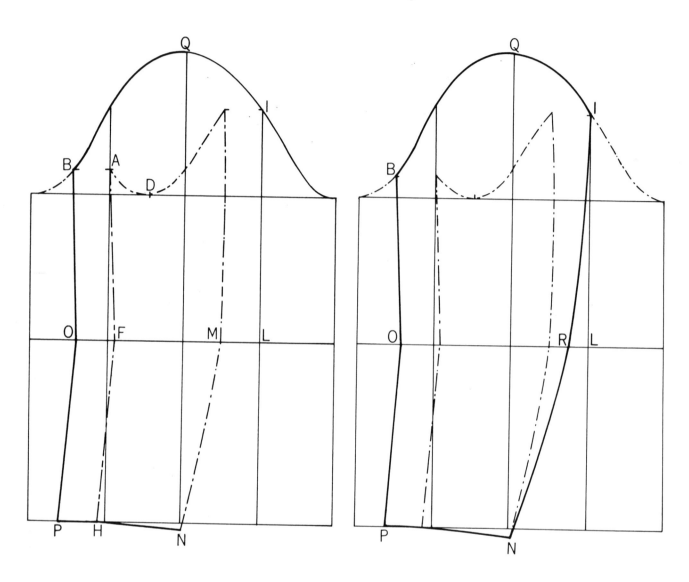

Upper Sleeve

F to O = 2".
H to P = 2".
Connect B to O and O to P with straight line to
   finish inseam.
Connect P to H to N to finish cuff.
Cap of upper sleeve is curve between B and Q and I.

L to R = 1".
Connect I to R with hip curve ruler.
Connect R to N with hip curve ruler to finish
   upper sleeve.

NOTES

SEMI-RAGLAN SLEEVE

Note: The average cuff measurement is 11"–12". This may be changed according to your design.

Three-Piece Sleeve

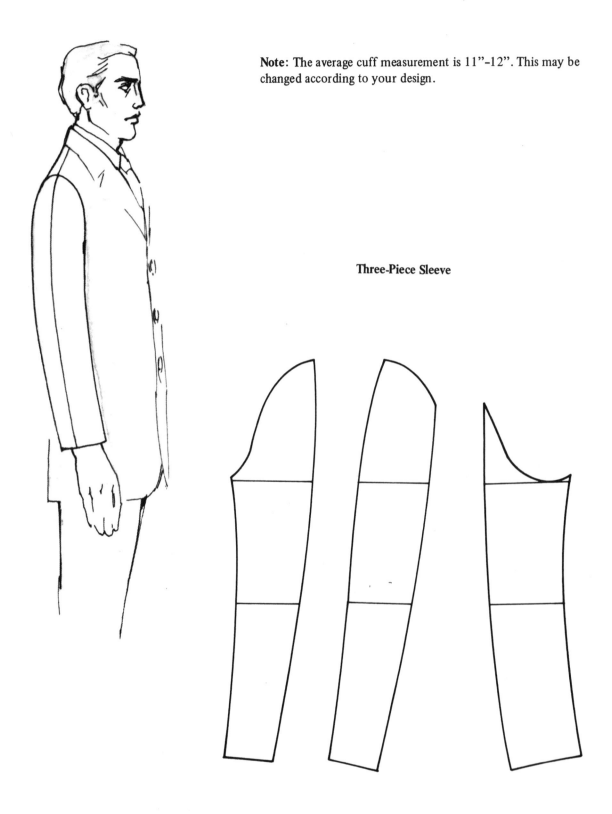

Upper Sleeve

Under Sleeve

SEMI-RAGLAN SLEEVE

DIAGRAM A

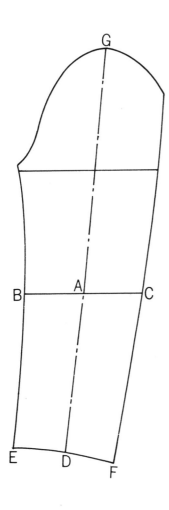

DIAGRAM B

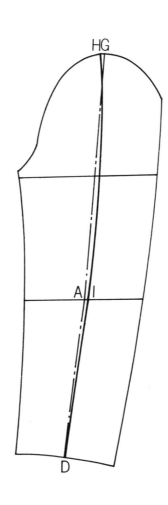

DIAGRAM C

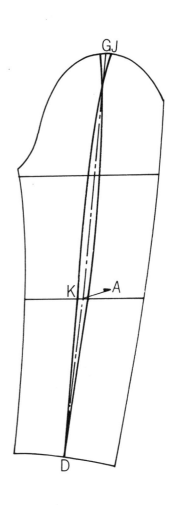

Outline upper sleeve.
Indicate elbow line.
A = 1/2 B to C.
D = 1/2 E to F.
G = center top of cap.
Connect G to A and A to D with
   straight line.

G to H = 1/4".
A to I = 1/8".
Connect H to I with hip curve ruler.
Connect I to D with straight line.

G to J = 1/4".
A to K = 1/8".
Connect J to K with hip curve ruler.
Connect K to D with straight line,
   to finish three-piece sleeve.

BASIC RAGLAN SLEEVE

DIAGRAM A—Basic Raglan Sleeve

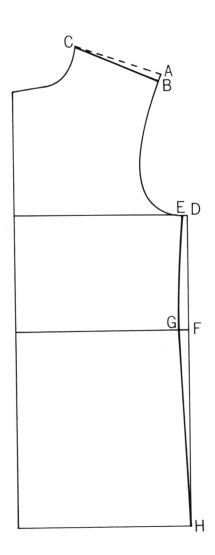

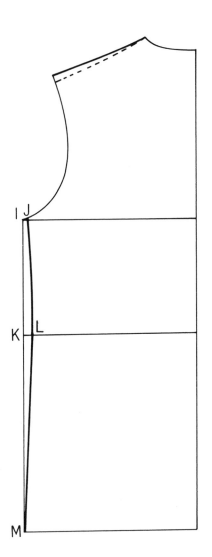

Outline jacket sloper, front and back.

Front Jacket Shoulder

A = shoulder at armhole.

A to B = 1/2".

C = shoulder at neck.

Connect B to C with straight line.

Remove A to B to C.

New shoulder line C to B.

Back Jacket Shoulder

Add to the back shoulder the amount removed from the front shoulder (see diagram).

Front Jacket Side Seam

D = side seam at chest line.

D to E = 1/4".

F to G = 1/2".

Connect E to G with hip curve ruler.

Connect G to H with straight line.

Back Jacket Side Seam

I = side seam at chest line.

I to J = 1/4".

K to L = 1/2".

Connect J to L with hip curve ruler.

Connect L to M with straight line.

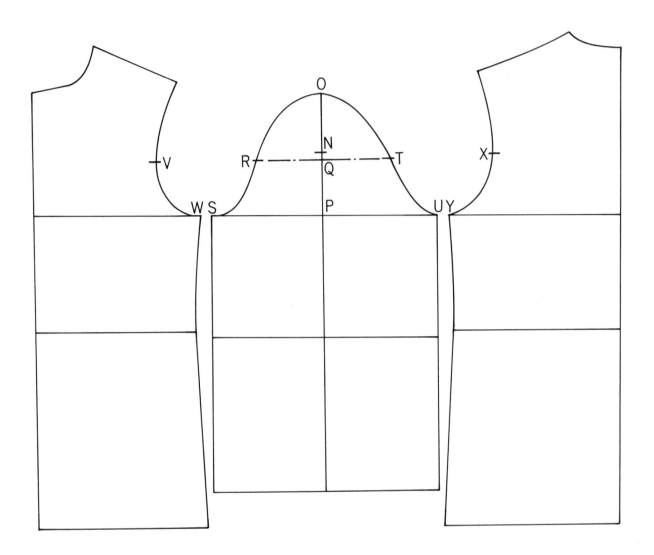

Diagram B

Sleeve
N = 1/2 O to P.
N to Q = 3/8".
Square off Q to R.
Square off Q to T.
S and U = armhole at inseam.
Cross mark at R and T.

Front Jacket Armhole
W to V = S to R.

Back Jacket Armhole
Y to X = U to T.

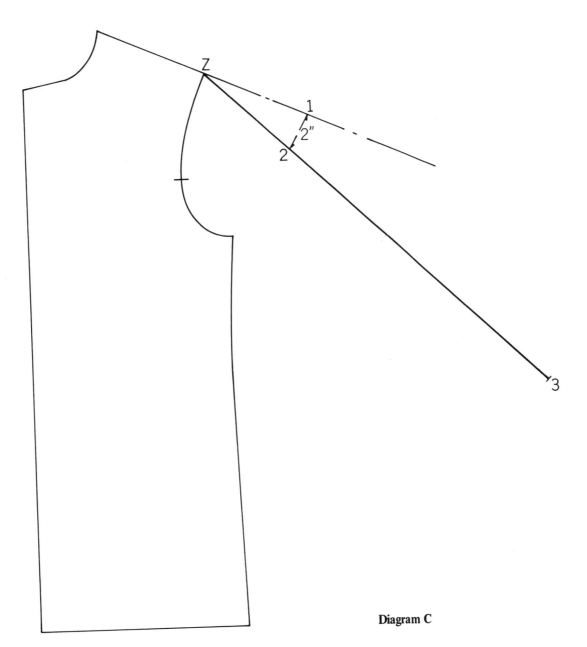

Diagram C

Front Raglan Sleeve

Extend shoulder line 10".
Z to 1 = 6".
1 to 2 = 2".
Z to 2 = 6".
Connect Z to 2 to 3.
Z to 3 = full sleeve length.

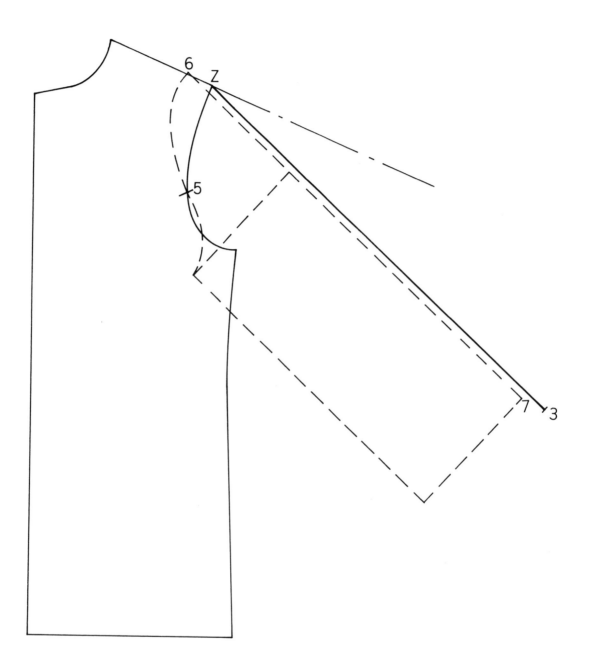

Diagram D

5 = point where cross mark R and V meet.
Bring sleeve points 6 to 7 parallel with Z to 3.

DIAGRAM—Basic Raglan Sleeve E

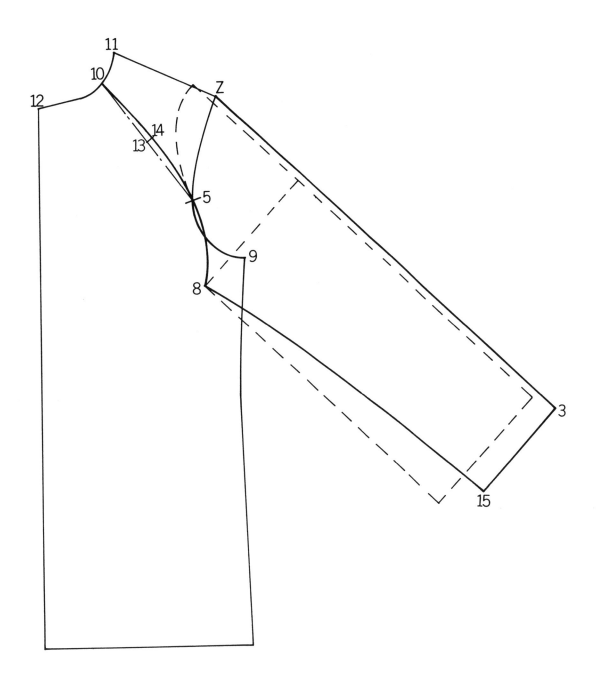

Diagram E

Outline 5 to 8.
Outline 5 to 9.
10 = 1/3 11 to 12.
Connect 5 to 10 with straight line as a guide.
13 = 1/2 10 to 5.
13 to 14 = 1/4".
Connect 10 to 14 to 5 with hip curve ruler.
3 to 15 = 6".
Connect 8 to 15 with hip curve ruler.

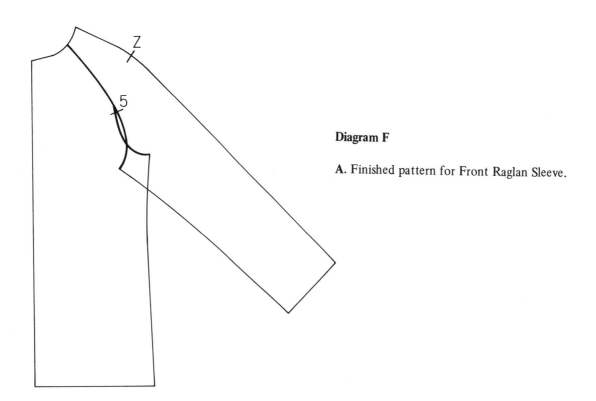

Diagram F

A. Finished pattern for Front Raglan Sleeve.

B. To give more action-ease use following
procedure.
   1. A = 1/2 B to C.
      B to D = 1/2" for ease.
   2. Slash 5 to 2.
      Bring B to O as diagram shows.
   3. Connect D to C to finish sleeve.

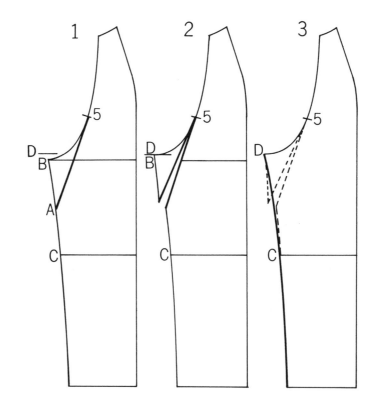

DIAGRAM–Basic Raglan Sleeve G

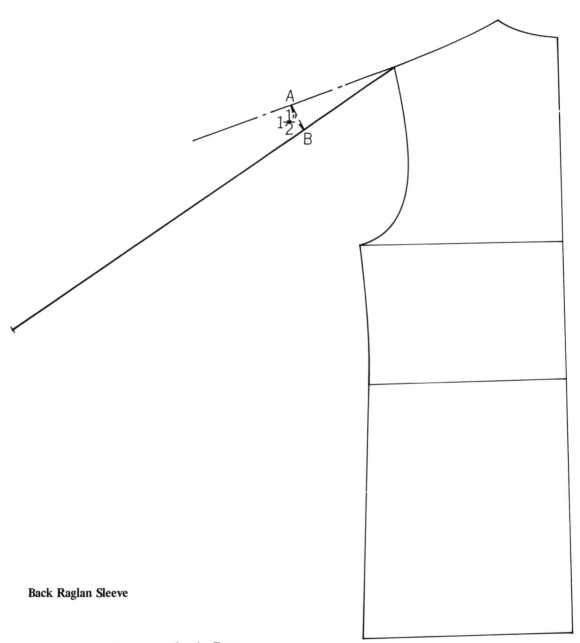

Back Raglan Sleeve

Procedure is the same as for the Front
Raglan Sleeve. Change measurement
between A to B, 1 1/2".

RAGLAN SLEEVE VARIATION

Same procedure as Basic Raglan Sleeve Procedure except for change found in Diagram: A to B = 1/2" deleting space area. Connect B to C.

DIAGRAM–Raglan Sleeve Variation

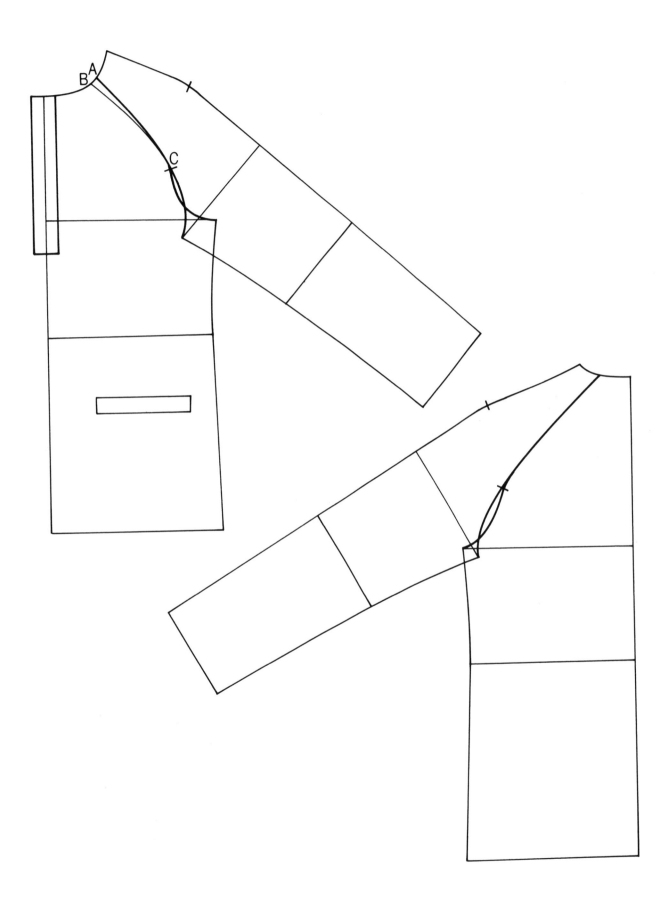

ONE-PIECE RAGLAN SLEEVE

Same as Basic Raglan Sleeve Procedure except front and back sleeve pattern pieces must be placed together at over-arm seam to create shoulder dart (as shown). Points A to B will then create a straight line from shoulder to wrist.

DIAGRAM-One-Piece Raglan Sleeve

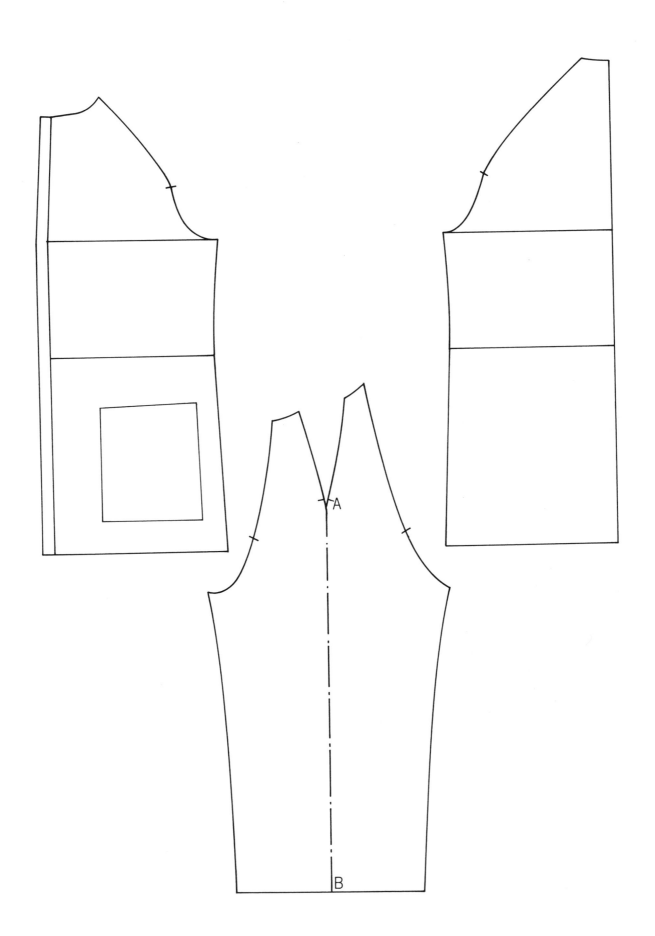

CUFF DESIGNS

A

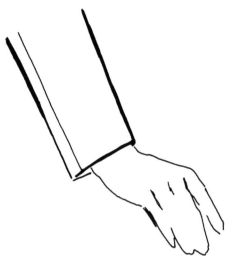

Basic Cuff

B

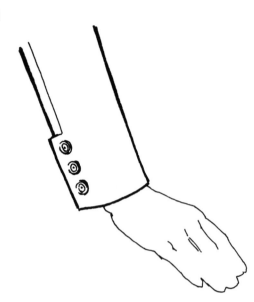

Vented Cuff

C

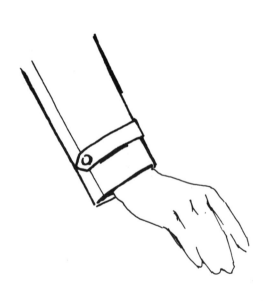

Button Strap Cuff

D

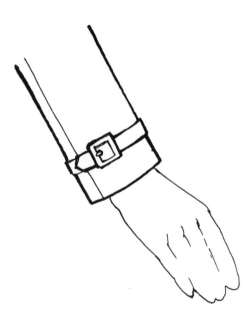

Buckle Strap Cuff

CUFF DESIGNS

E

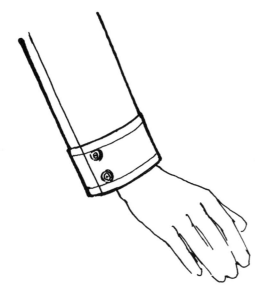

Barrel Cuff

F

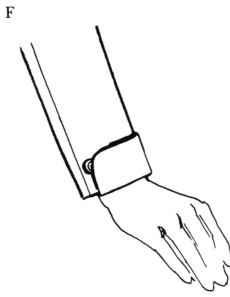

Semi-French Cuff

G

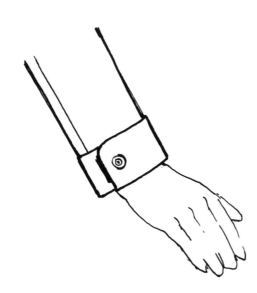

French Variation Cuff

H

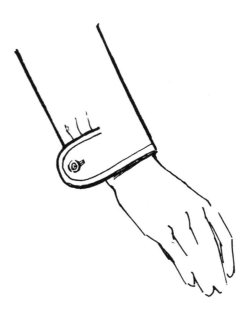

Tab Cuff

ROUND NECKLINE

A to B = 3/4" extension.
C is at neck point.
C to D = 1/2".
D to E = 3/4".
Connect E to B and D to A with straight line to
    establish new center front.
F = shoulder at neck.
Finish neckline with sleigh curve.

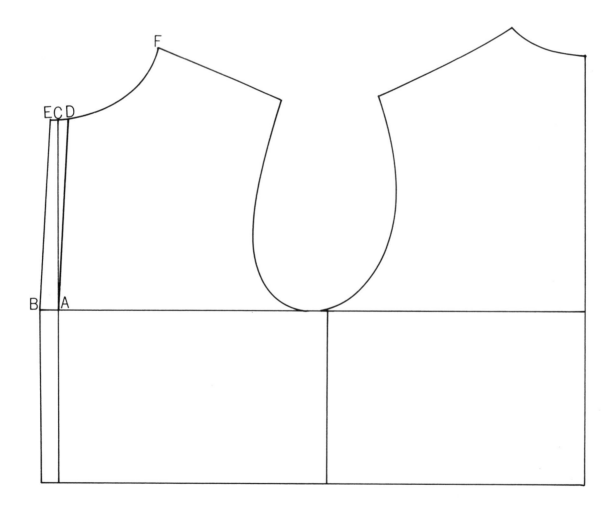

SQUARE NECKLINE

A to B = 3/4" extension.
C is at neck point.
C to D = 1/2".
C to E = 2".
Connect D to A to establish new center front.
F is shoulder at neck.
Square off E to G.
Connect F to G with straight line.
G to H = 1/2".
Square off I to J for 3/4" extension.

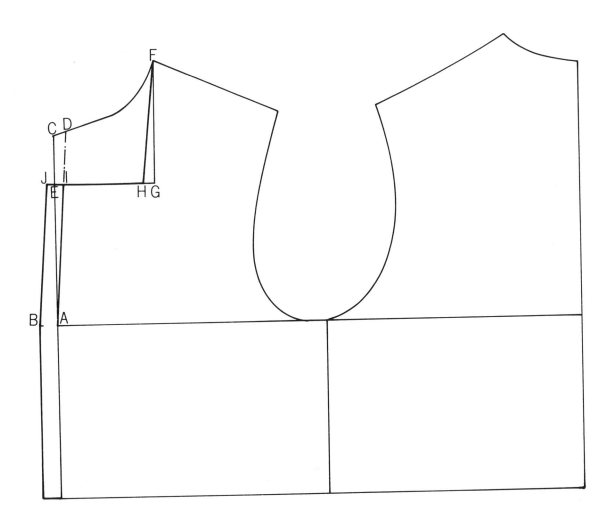

V-NECKLINE

A to B = 3/4" extension.
B to C = 1".
D is shoulder at neck.
Connect C to D.
E = 1/2 C to D.
E to F = 1/4".
Connect D to F and F to C with hip curve ruler to finish
  neckline.

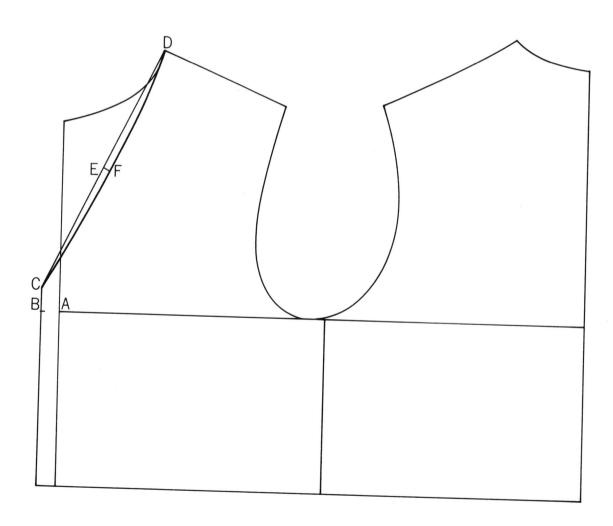

BOAT NECKLINE

Front Panel

A = neck point.
A to B = 3/8".
C = shoulder at armhole.
C to D = 1".
E = shoulder at neck.
D to F = 1/2".
F to G = 2".
Connect B to G with hip curve ruler.
Blend in armhole from F to finish front neck and armhole.

Back Panel

H = center back at neck.
H to I = 3/8".
J = shoulder at neck.
K = shoulder at armhole.
K to L = 1".
Connect J to L with same curve as J to K.
L to M = 2".
Connect M to I with hip curve ruler.
Connect L to K with finish back panel.

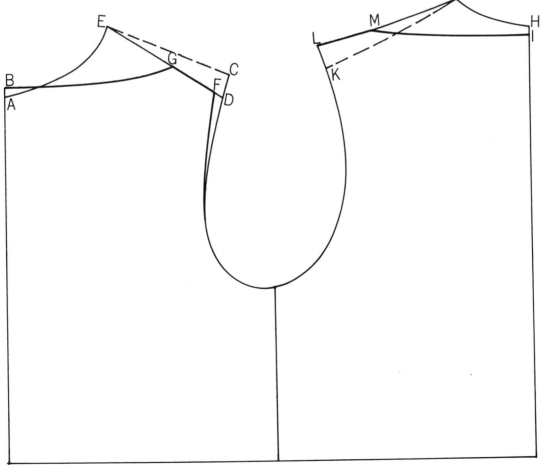

BASIC BANDED COLLAR VARIATION

Note: Because your basic sloper is drafted for the notched collar jacket, the following adjustments are needed for a new front neckline:

A = shoulder point at neck.
Extend 3/8" to B.
C = neckpoint.
C to D = 3/8".
E at chest center front.
>   Connect D to E to finish new center front.
>   E to F = 3/4" for extension.
>   Square off from D to G = 3/4" for extension.
>   Connect G to F with straight line.
>   Connect B to D with sleigh curve to finish new neckline.

Back Neckline
Extend H to I = 3/8".
J to K = 1/8".
>   Connect I to K with sleigh curve ruler to finish back neckline.

Collar
Diagram A
Draw line 10" long.

Diagram B
1 to 2 = 1/2 front neck measurement.
2 to 3 = 1/2 back neck measurement.
3 to 4 = collar stand 1 1/2".
1 to 5 = collar stand 1 1/2".
Connect 1 to 3
Square up from 3 to 4.
Square up from 1 to 5.
Connect 5 to 4.

Diagram C
5 to 6 = 1/2".

Diagram D
Connect 6 to 1 to finish banded collar.

DIAGRAM–Basic Banded Collar Variation A, B, C, D

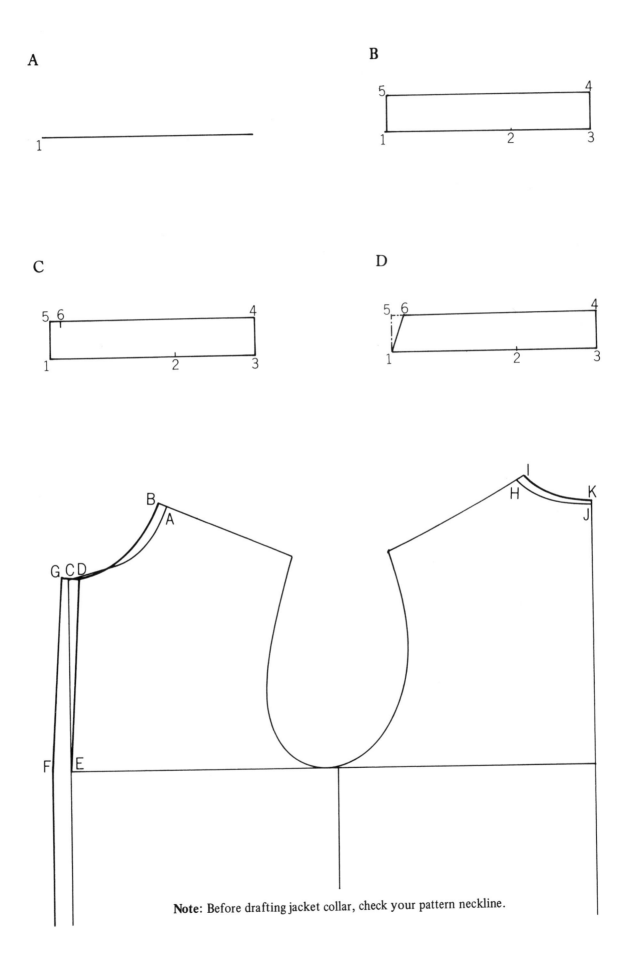

A

1

B

5   4

1   2   3

C

5 6   4

1   2   3

D

5 6   4

1   2   3

B
A
G C D
F E

I
H   K
J

Note: Before drafting jacket collar, check your pattern neckline.

BANDED COLLAR VARIATION

Outline your jacket sloper.

Neckline
A to B = 4".
C = shoulder at neck.
Connect C to B.
D = 1/2 B to C.
D to E = 1/4".
Connect C to E to B with hip curve ruler to finish neckline.

Collar
The banded collar variation is similar to the basic banded collar with the exception of a slight curve from shoulder to center front.

Diagram A
Draw 10" line.
Square up 1 to 2 = 1/4".

Diagram B
2 to 3 = 1/2 front neck measurement.
Connect 2 to 3 with hip curve ruler.
3 to 4 = 1/2 back neck measurement.
Square up 4 to 5 = 1 1/2".

Diagram C
Square up from 2 to 6 = 1 1/2".
3 to 7 = 1 1/2".

Diagram D
Connect 5 to 7 with straight line.
Connect 7 to 6 with the same curve as 2 to 3 to finish collar.

DIAGRAM—Banded Collar Variation A, B, C, D

A

B

C

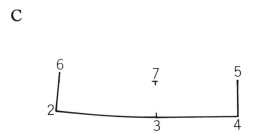

D

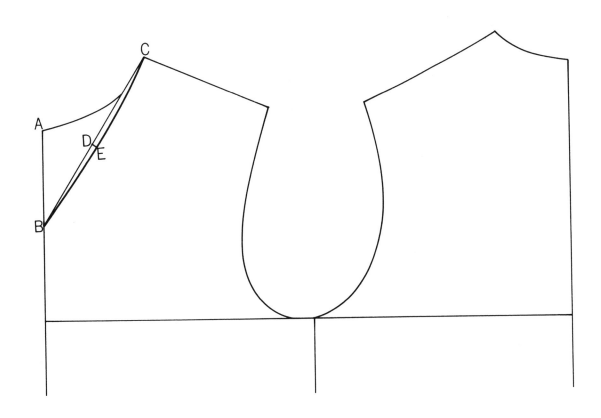

MANDARIN COLLAR VARIATION

Outline basic jacket sloper.

Neckline

The neckline is completed by using the same method as the
   banded collar.

Collar

Diagram A

Draw 10" line.

Diagram B

Square up 1 to 2 = 3/4".

Diagram C

2 to 3 = 1/2 front neck measurement.
Connect 2 to 3 with hip curve ruler.
3 to 4 = 1/2 back neck measurement.

Diagram D

Square up 4 to 5 = 1 3/4".
Square up 2 to 6 = 1 3/4".

Diagram E

3 to 7 = 1 3/4".
Connect 5 to 7 with straight line.
Connect 7 to 6 with same curve as 2 to 3 to finish mandarin
   collar.

DIAGRAM—Mandarin Collar Variation A, B, C, D, E

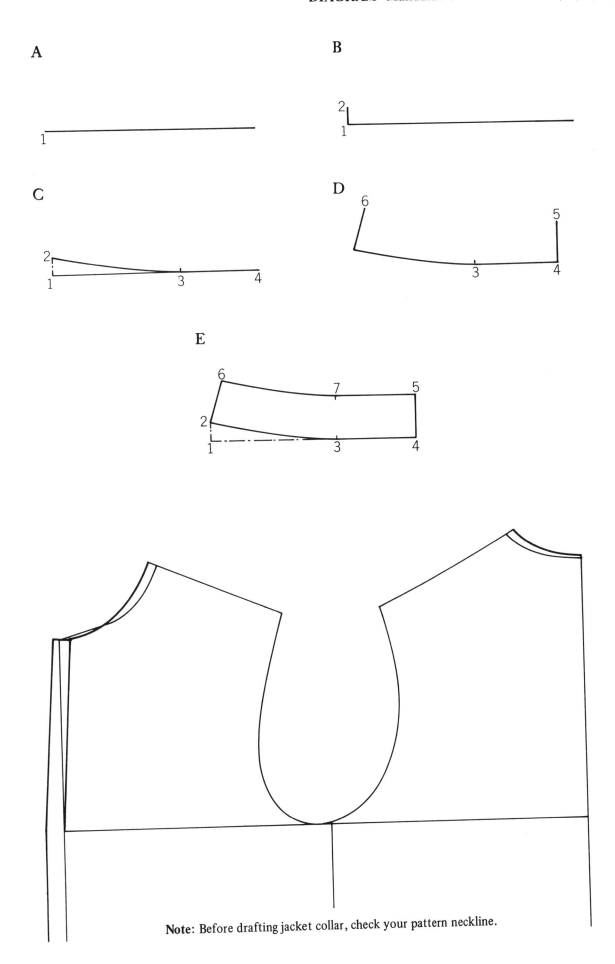

Note: Before drafting jacket collar, check your pattern neckline.

174

FUNNEL COLLAR VARIATION

Outline your jacket sloper.

Neckline
A to B = 1/2".
Connect B to C.
B to D = 1/2".
D to E = 3/4".
C to F = 3/4" for extension.
Connect D to C and E to F.
G to H = 1/4".
Connect H to D to E with sleigh curve.
I to J = 1/4".
Connect J to K with sleigh curve to finish neckline.

Collar

Diagram A
Draw line 10" long.

Diagram B
Square up 1 to 2 = 2".

Diagram C
2 to 3 = 1/2 front neck measurement.
Connect 2 to 3 with sleigh curve.
3 to 4 = 1/2 back neck measurement.

Diagram D
Square up 4 to 5 = 1 3/4".
Square up 2 to 6 = 1 3/4".

Diagram E
3 to 7 = 1 3/4".
Connect 5 to 7 with straight line.
Connect 7 to 6 with same curve as 3 to 2 to finish funnel
    collar.

DIAGRAM—Funnel Collar Variation A, B, C, D, E

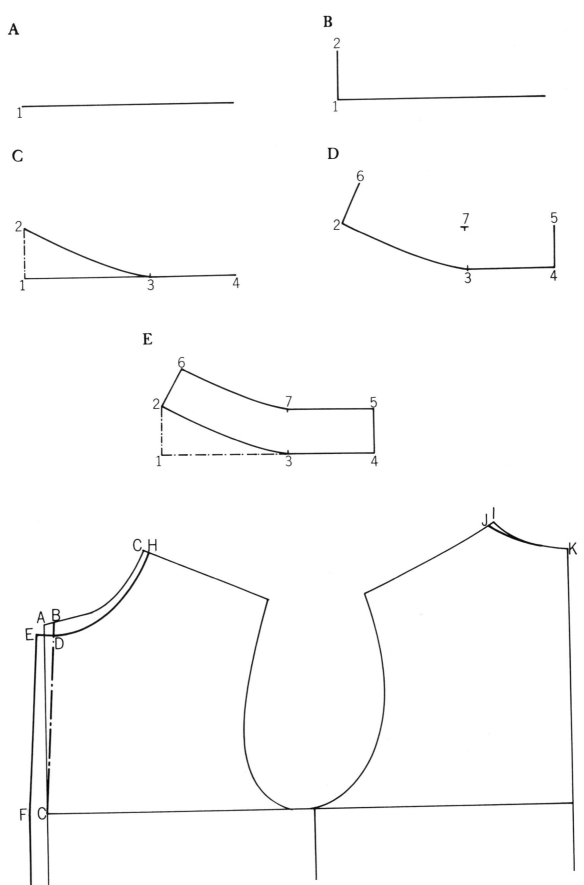

Note: Before drafting jacket collar, check your pattern neckline.

CONVERTIBLE COLLAR VARIATION

Outline your jacket sloper.

Tab

A to B = 1/2".

Connect B to C to establish new center front.

Width of tab = 2".

C to D = 1".

B to E = 1".

B to F = 1".

C to G = 1".

Square off B to E.

Connect E to D to G to F to finish tab.

Neckline

The neckline is completed by using the same method as the banded collar.

Collar

Diagram A

Draw line 10" long.

Diagram B

Square up 1 to 2 = 1/2".

2 to 3 = 1/2 front neck measurement.

Connect 2 to 3 with hip curve ruler.

3 to 4 = 1/2 back nect measurement.

Diagram C

Square up 4 to 5 = 3 1/8".

1 to 6 = 4 to 5.

Extend 6 to 7 = 1 1/2".

6 to 8 = 1/4".

Diagram D

9 = 1/2 5 to 6.

Connect 2 to 7 to 10 = 3 1/2".

Connect 9 to 8 to 10 with hip curve ruler to finish
  convertible collar.

DIAGRAM–Convertible Collar Variation A, B, C, D

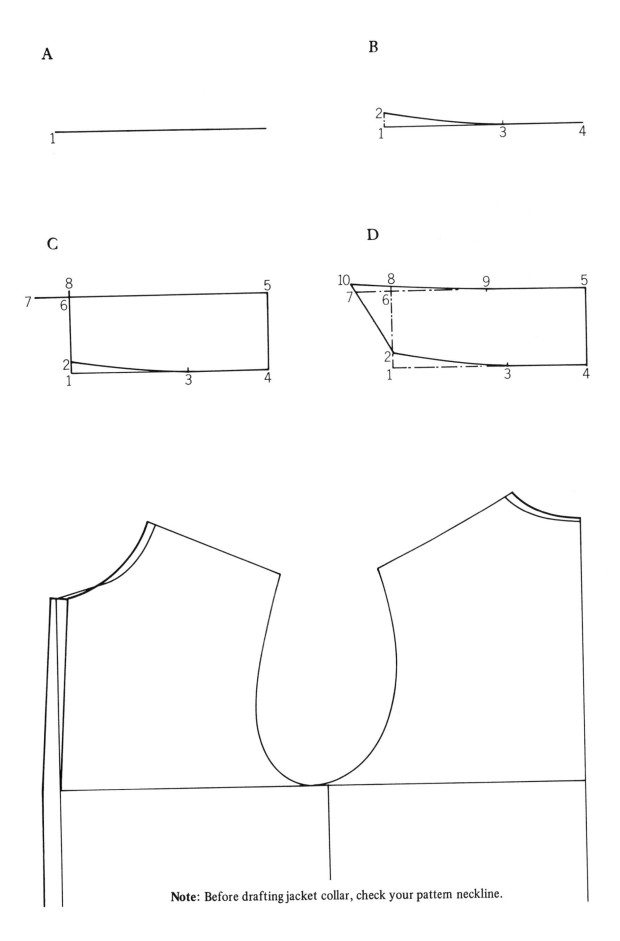

A

B

C

D

Note: Before drafting jacket collar, check your pattern neckline.

OPEN NECK CONVERTIBLE COLLAR VARIATION

Outline basic jacket sloper.

Neckline
A = neck point.
A to B = 1/2".
C = center front at chest line.
Connect B to C to establish new center front.
D = 1/3 B to D.
E = shoulder at neck.
H = 1/3 E to D.
H = starting point for collar - place crossmark.

Collar
Diagram A
Draw 10" line.

Diagram B
1 to 2 = 2/3 front neck measurement.
2 to 3 = 1/2 back neck measurement.
Square up 3 to 4 = 2 1/4".
Square up 1 to 5 = 2 1/4".
Connect 4 to 5.

Diagram C
Extend 5 to 6 = 1 1/2".
Extend 5 to 7 = 1/4".

Diagram D
8 = 1/2 4 to 7.
Connect 1 to 6 to 9 = 3 1/2".
Connect 8 to 7 to 9 with hip curve ruler to finish
    convertible collar.

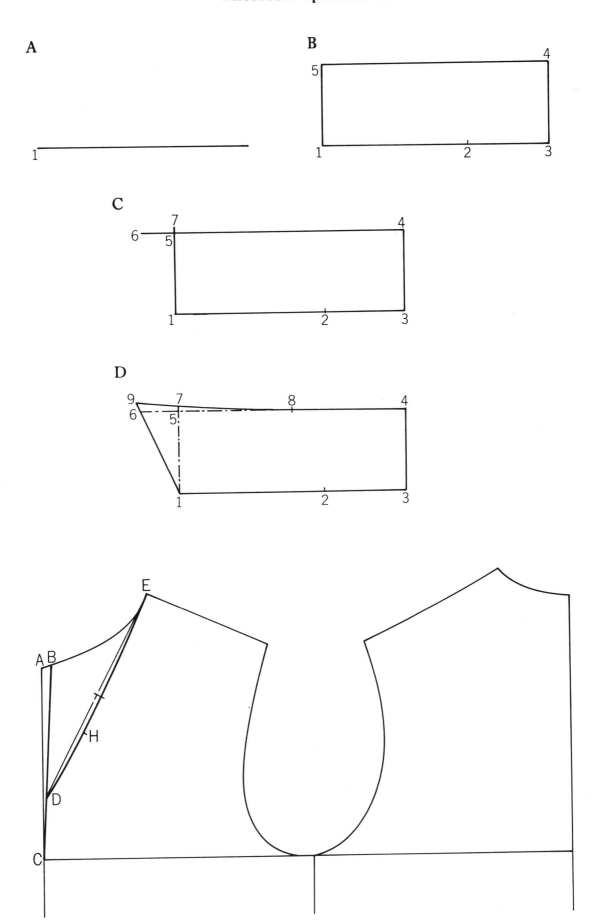

CONTINENTAL COLLAR VARIATION

Neckline
The neckline is completed by using the same method as the banded collar.

Collar
Diagram A
Draw 10" line.

Diagram B
Square up 1 to 2 = 3/4".
2 to 3 = 1/2 front neck measurement.
3 to 4 = 1/2 back neck measurement.
Square up 4 to 5.

Diagram C
Square up 2 to 6 = 3/4".
Connect 5 to 6 with straight line.

Diagram D
5 to 7 = 1 3/4".
6 to 8 = 1 3/4".
Connect 8 to 7.

Diagram E
Extend 8 to 9 = 1 1/2".
Extend 8 to 10 = 1/2".

Diagram F
11 = 1/2 8 to 7.
6 to 9 to 12 = 3 1/2".
Connect 11 to 10 to 12 with hip curve ruler to finish
    continental collar.

DIAGRAM—Continental Collar Variation A, B, C, D, E, F

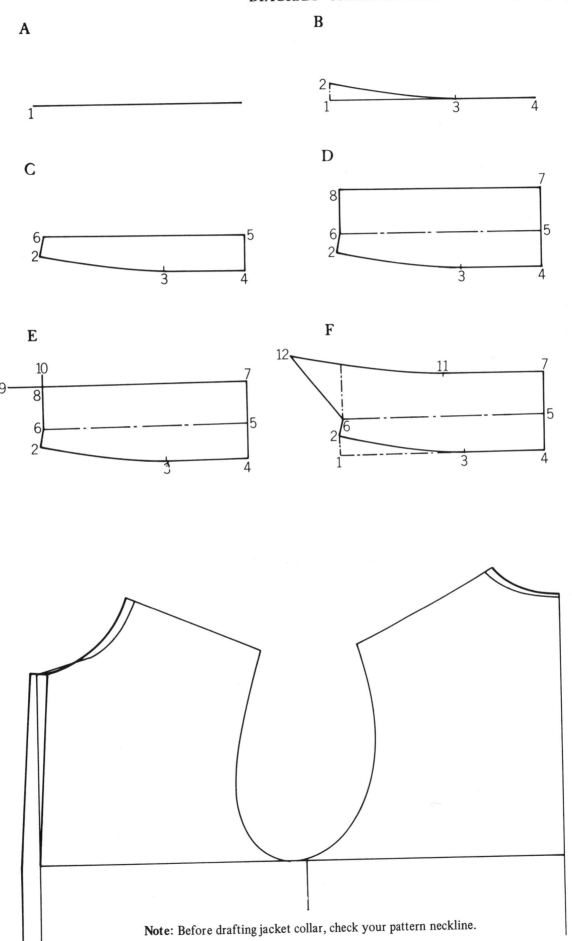

Note: Before drafting jacket collar, check your pattern neckline.

SHIRT COLLAR VARIATION

Outline basic jacket sloper.

Neckline
The neckline is completed by using the same method as the banded collar.

Collar
Diagram A
Draw 10" line.

Diagram B
Square up 1 to 2 = 1/2".
2 to 3 = 1/2 front neck measurement.
Connect 2 to 3 with hip curve ruler.
3 to 4 = 1/2 back neck measurement.

Diagram C
Square up 4 to 5 = 1 1/2".
3 to 7 = 1 1/2".
Square up 2 to 6.
6 to 9 = 3/4" for extension.
2 to 8 = 3/4" for extension.
Connect all points as shown in diagram.

Diagram D
5 to 10 = 1/4".
Connect 6 to 10 with straight line.

Diagram E
10 to 11 = 1/4".
Connect 6 to 11 with same curve as 5 to 7 to 6.

Diagram F
11 to 12 = 1 7/8".
6 to 13 = 10 to 12.
13 to 14 = 1".
13 to 15 = 1/2".

Diagram G
16 = 1/2 12 to 13.
Connect 6 to 14 to 17 = 4".
Connect 16 to 15 to 17 with hip curve ruler to finish dress
    collar variation.

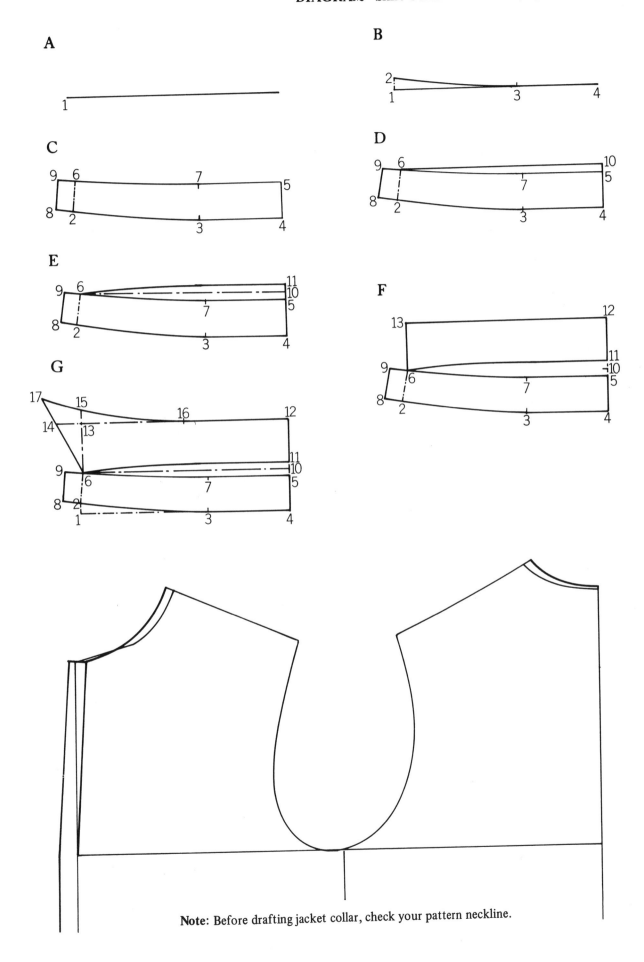

A

1

B

2
1   3   4

C

9 6   7   5
8 2   3   4

D

9 6   10
      7   5
8 2   3   4

E

9 6   11
                              10
      7   5
8 2   3   4

F

13   12
9 6   11
                             10
      7   5
8 2   3   4

G

17 15   16   12
14 13
9 6   11
                             10
      7   5
8 2
1   3   4

Note: Before drafting jacket collar, check your pattern neckline.

DRESS SHIRT COLLAR VARIATION

Outline basic jacket sloper.

Neckline
The neckline is completed by using the same method as the banded collar.

Collar
Diagram A
Draw line 10" long.

Diagram B
Square up 1 to 2 = 1 1/4".
2 to 3 = 1/2 front neck measurement.
Connect 2 to 3 with sleigh curve.
3 to 4 = 1/2 back neck measurement.
Square up 4 to 5 = 1 1/2".
Square up 2 to 6 = 1 1/4".

Diagram C
3 to 7 = 1 1/2".
2 to 8 = 3/4" for extension.
6 to 9 = 3/4" for extension.
Connect as shown in diagram.

Diagram D
Connect 5 to 7 with straight line.
Connect 7 to 6 with sleigh curve.

Diagram E
5 to 10 = Square off from 10 to 6
Connect 10 to 6 with straight line.

Diagram F
10 to 11 = 5 to 10
Connect 11 to 6 with same curve as 5 to 7 to 6.

Diagram G
11 to 12 = 1 3/4".
6 to 13 = 10 to 12.

Diagram H
Extend 13 to 14.
6 to 14 = 4" to finish dress shirt collar.

DIAGRAM—Dress Shirt Collar Variation A, B, C, D, E, F, G, H

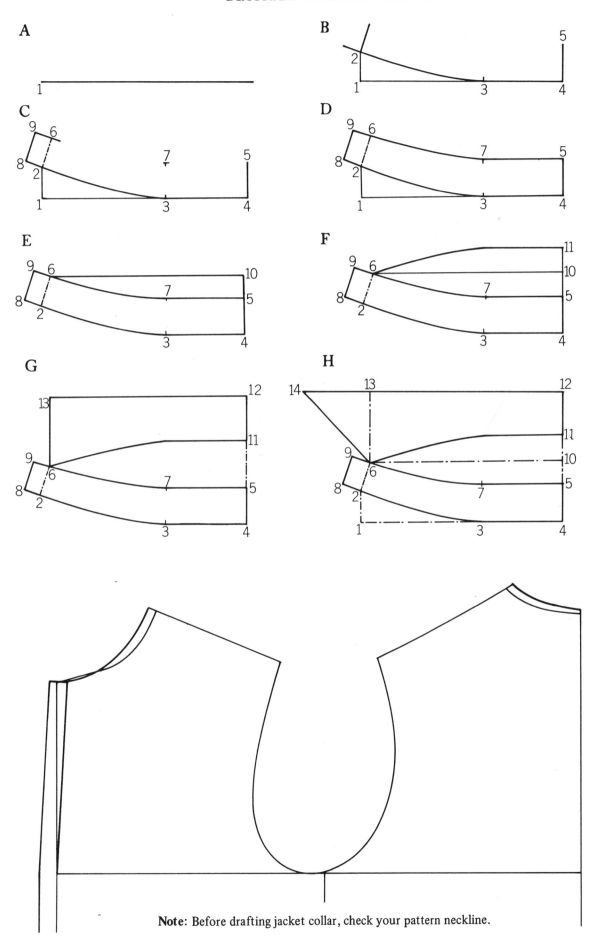

Note: Before drafting jacket collar, check your pattern neckline.

COLLAR PARTS AND NOTCH COLLAR SIZE VARIATIONS CHART

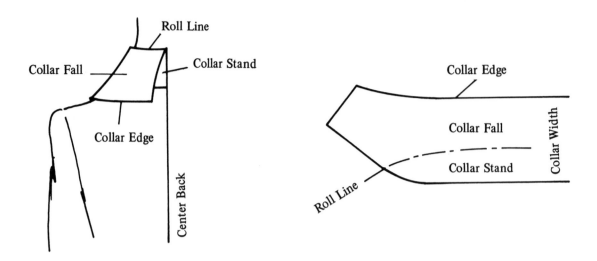

COMMERCIALLY USED NOTCHED COLLAR SIZE VARIATIONS

Shifting is a procedure which will give the correct collar-edge measurement.
This will give a proper fit to the notched collar.

NOTE: In Size Charts A, B1, and B2 breakpoint = 2" above waist.

A. Both stand and collar fall change 1/8". Amount of shift is 1/2" in all sizes.

Collar Stand	1-1/8	1-1/4	1-3/8	1-1/2
Collar Fall	1-5/8	1-3/4	1-7/8	2
Collar Width	2-3/4	3	3-1/4	3-1/2
Shift	1/2	1/2	1/2	1/2

B1. Stand remains the same throughout all sizes. Collar fall gain is 1/8" in each size. Shift will then gain 1/8" also in all sizes.

Collar Stand	1-1/8	1-1/8	1-1/8	1-1/8
Collar Fall	1-5/8	1-3/4	1-7/8	2
Collar Width	2-3/4	2-7/8	3	3-1/8
Shift	1/2	5/8	3/4	7/8

NOTCH COLLAR SIZE VARIATIONS CHART

B2. Same as B1, except stand measurement is higher. Shift also changes 1/8" in all sizes.

Collar Stand	1-1/4	1-1/4	1-1/4	1-1/4
Collar Fall	1-3/4	1-7/8	2	2-1/2
Collar Width	3	3-1/8	3-1/4	3-3/4
Shift	1/2	5/8	3/4	7/8

C. Use the following chart when breakpoint on Single-Breasted Jacket changes due to styling; e.g., breakpoint 2" above waistline requires 5/16" shift in collar, etc.

Collar Stand	1-1/8	1-1/8	1-1/8	1-1/8	1-1/8	1-1/8
Collar Fall	1-5/8	1-5/8	1-5/8	1-5/8	1-5/8	1-5/8
Collar Width	2-3/4	2-3/4	2-3/4	2-3/4	2-3/4	2-3/4
Shift	5/16	6/16	7/16	1/2	9/16	5/8
Above W.L.	2	3	4	5	6	7

D. Use the following chart when breakpoint on Double-Breasted Jacket changes due to styling; e.g., breakpoint 2" above waistline requires 5/16" shift in collar, etc.

Collar Stand	1-1/8	1-1/8	1-1/8	1-1/8	1-1/8	1-1/8
Collar Fall	1-5/8	1-5/8	1-5/8	1-5/8	1-5/8	1-5/8
Collar Width	2-3/4	2-3/4	2-3/4	2-3/4	2-3/4	2-3/4
Shift	3/8	7/16	1/2	9/16	5/8	11/16
Above W.L.	2	3	4	5	6	7

NOTCH COLLAR

DIAGRAM A

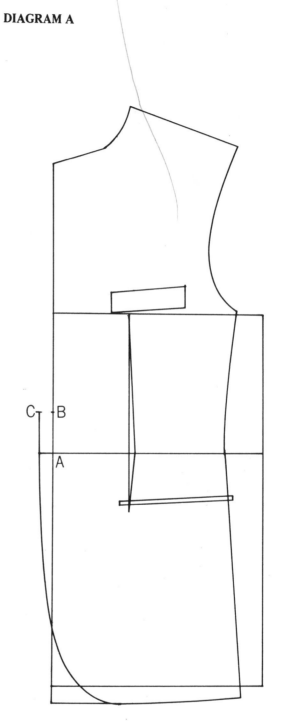

Measurement according to your design.
For example: collar stand = 1-1/8".
              collar fall = 1-5/8".
              collar width = 1-3/4".
              shift = 1/2".
See **Notch Collar Size Variation**, page 186.

A = waist at center front.
B = position of first button.
B to C = 3/4" for extension.
C = break point.

NOTCH COLLAR

DIAGRAM B

DIAGRAM C

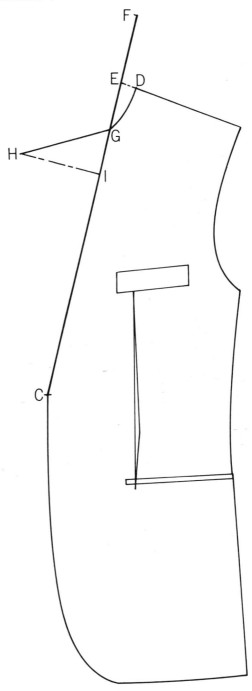

D = shoulder neck point.
D to E = collar stand.
Connect and extend C to E to establish roll line.
E to F = back neck measurement.

G = roll line at neck.
Extend G to H with straight line.
   neckline as a guide.
G to H is a straight line.
Square off point I to H for lapel width.

NOTCH COLLAR

DIAGRAM D

DIAGRAM E

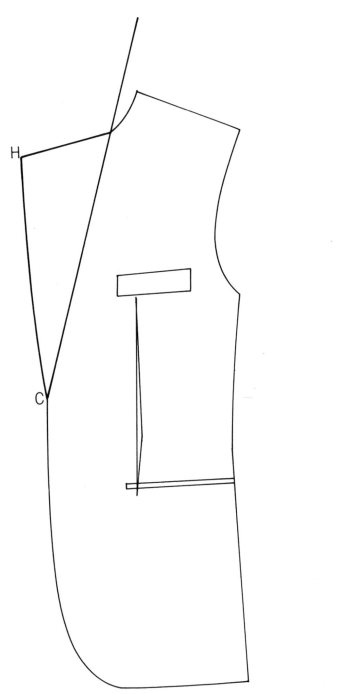

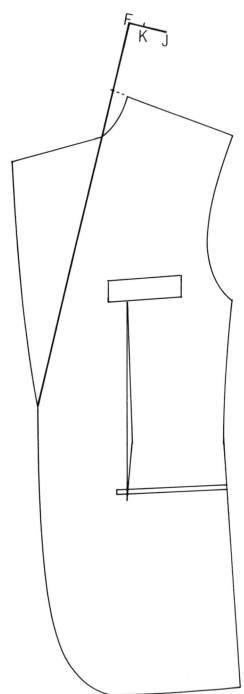

Connect H to C with hip curve ruler using deeper curve toward C.

Square off from point F.

F to K = shifting amount (see **Size Chart**, page 186).

K to J = collar stand.

NOTCH COLLAR

DIAGRAM F

DIAGRAM G

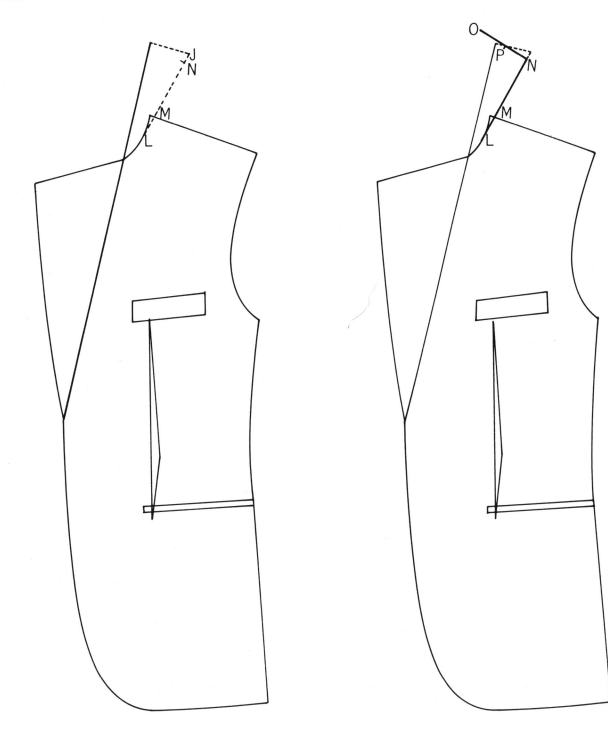

L = deepest section of neck.
Connect J to L.
M to N = back neck measurement.

Square from N.
N to P = collar stand.
P to O = collar fall.
N to O = collar width.

NOTCH COLLAR

DIAGRAM H

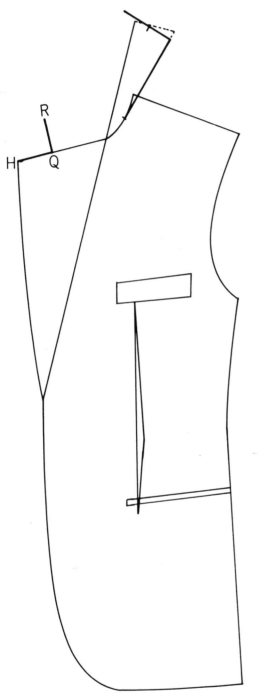

DIAGRAM I

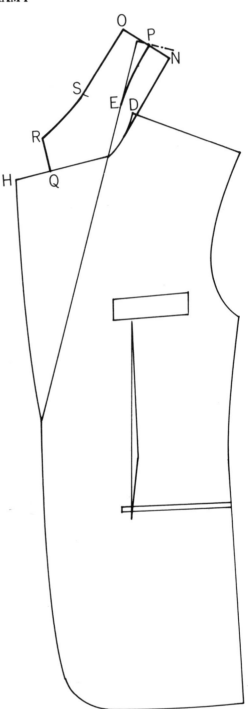

H to Q = length of notch.
Q to R = length and angle according to design.

Square off O to S.
S = extended line from shoulder.
Connect R to S with a straight line.
Blend in S to finish collar line.
Blend in at point E to finish roll line.

NOTCH COLLAR

Collar

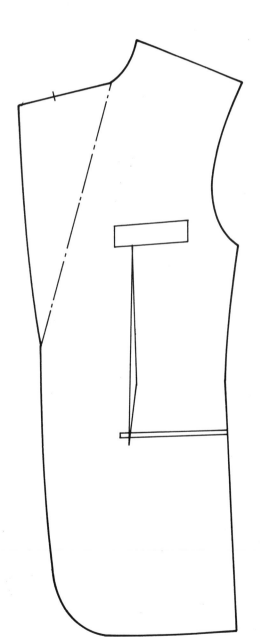

Jacket Front

NOTCH COLLAR DESIGN

(There are many variations of these collars.)

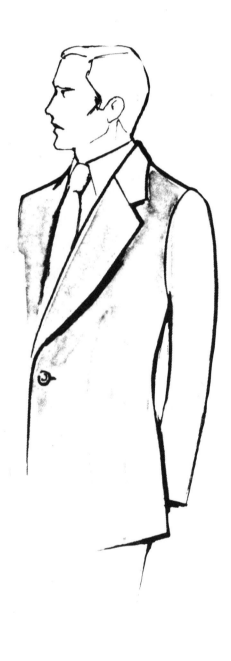

Basic Notch Collar

Clover Notch Collar

NOTCH COLLAR DESIGN

Semi-Peaked Notch Collar

Peaked Notch Collar

NOTCH COLLAR DESIGN

M Notch Collar

T Notch Collar

NOTCH COLLAR DESIGN

Shawl Collar

Notched shawl collar

NOTCH COLLAR DESIGN

Fish Mouth Notch Collar

L-Notch Collar

NOTES

CENTER VENTS

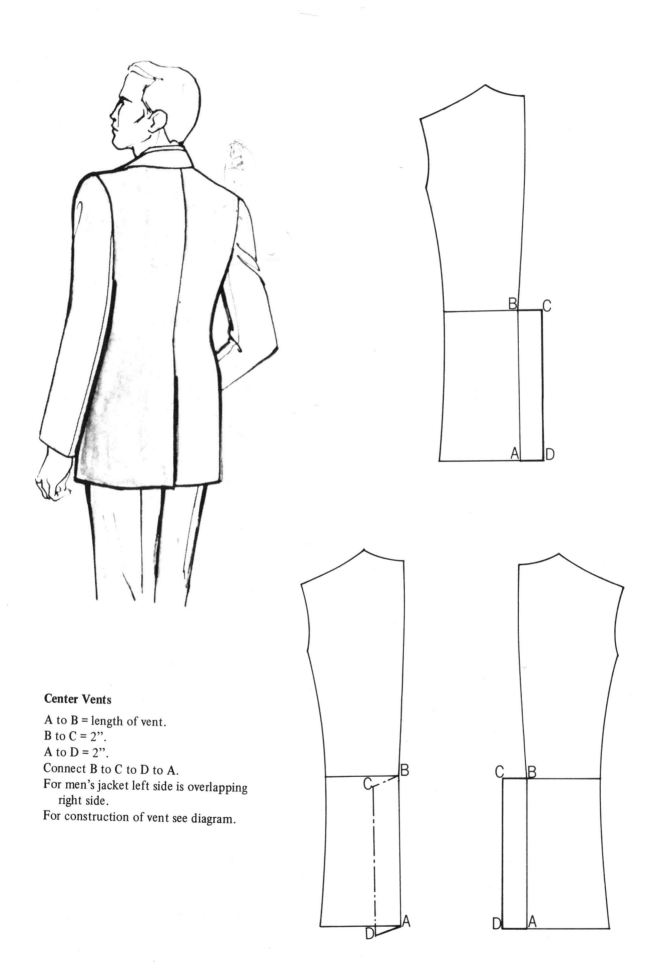

Center Vents

A to B = length of vent.
B to C = 2".
A to D = 2".
Connect B to C to D to A.
For men's jacket left side is overlapping right side.
For construction of vent see diagram.

SIDE VENTS

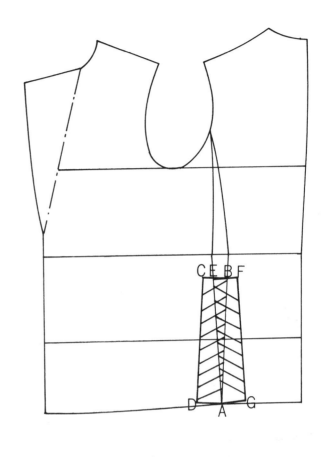

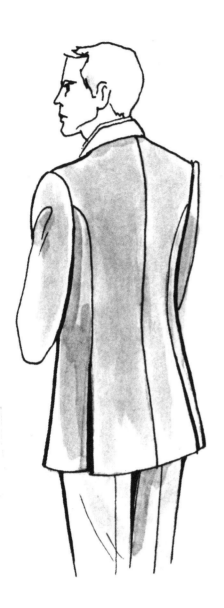

Side Vents

A = back side seam.
A to B = vent length.
B to D = 2".
A to C = 2".
Connect A to C, C to D, and D to B.
E to H = A to B.
E to F = 2".
H to G = 2".
Connect E to F, F to G, and G to H.
Center panel overlaps side panel.
For construction of vent see diagram.

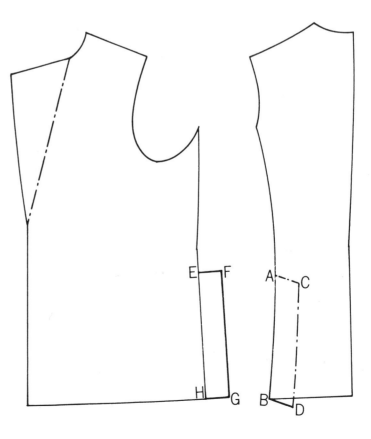

JACKET BACK VIEW, SET-IN BELT WITH DARTS VARIATION

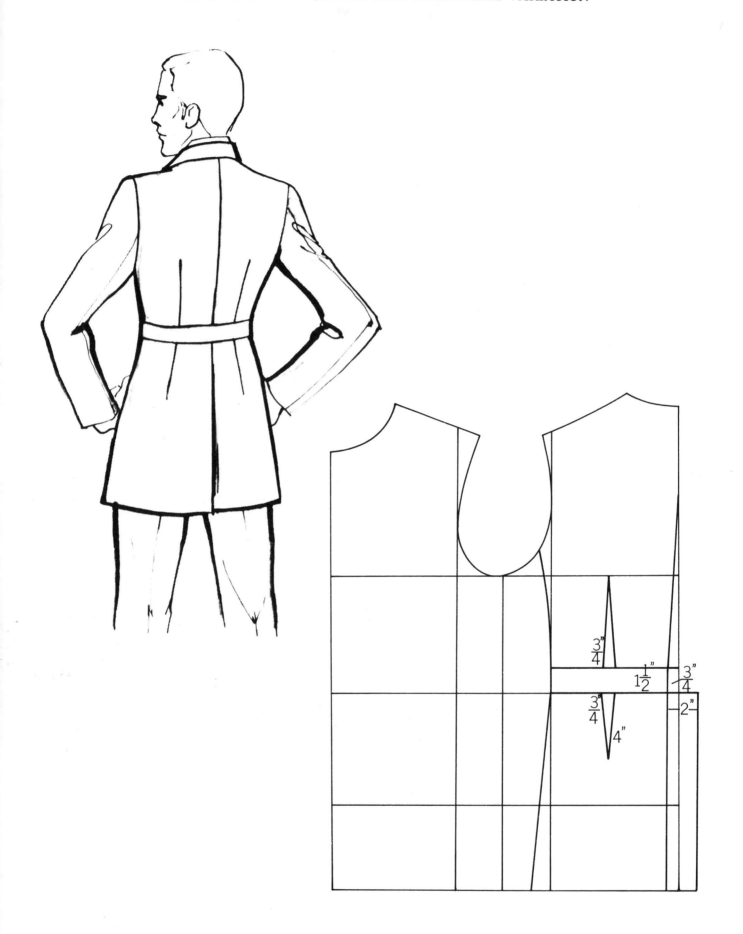

JACKET BACK VIEW, SET-IN BELT WITH DARTS VARIATION

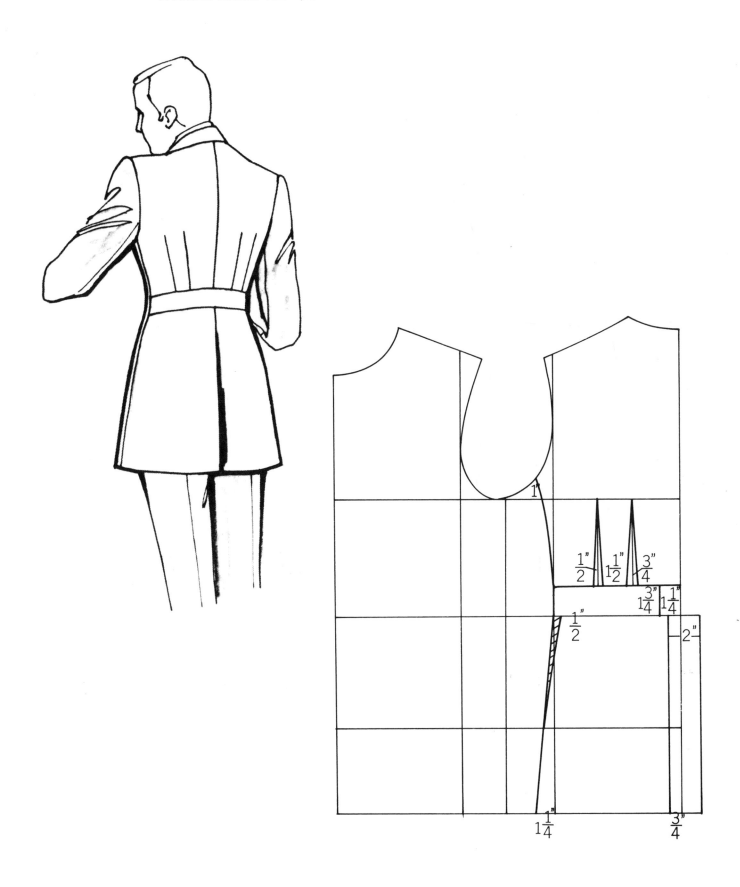

JACKET BACK VIEW, SET-IN BELT WITH PLEAT VARIATION

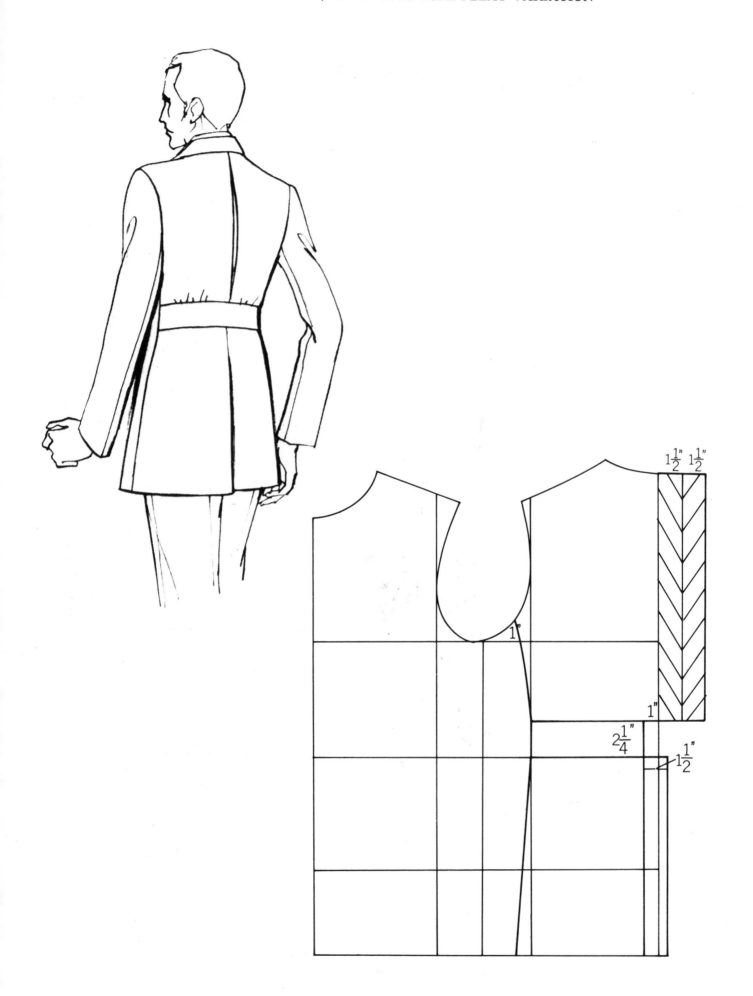

JACKET BACK VIEW, YOKE VARIATION

JACKET BACK VIEW, YOKE VARIATION

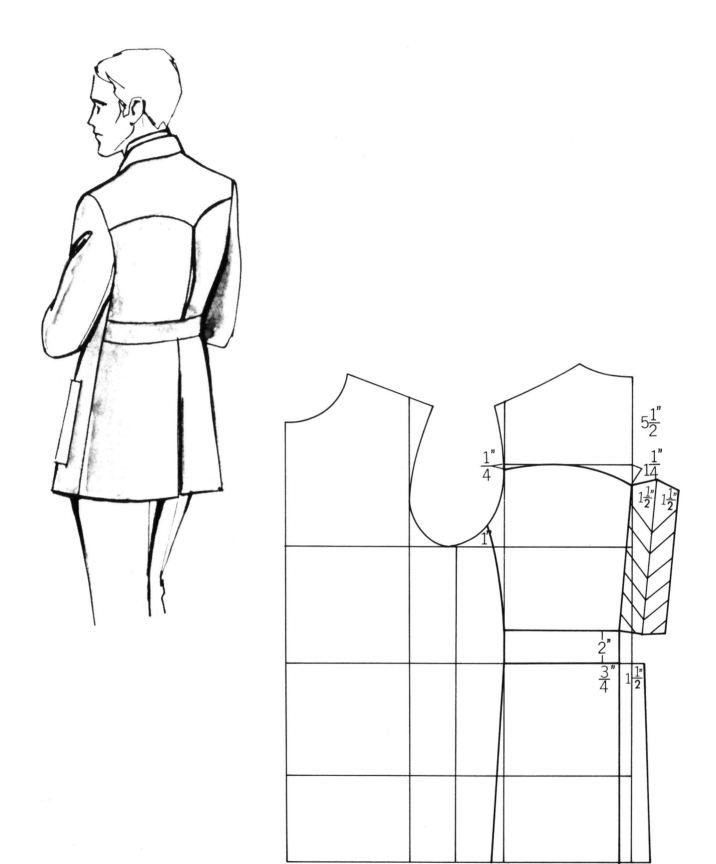

JACKET BACK VIEW, YOKE VARIATION

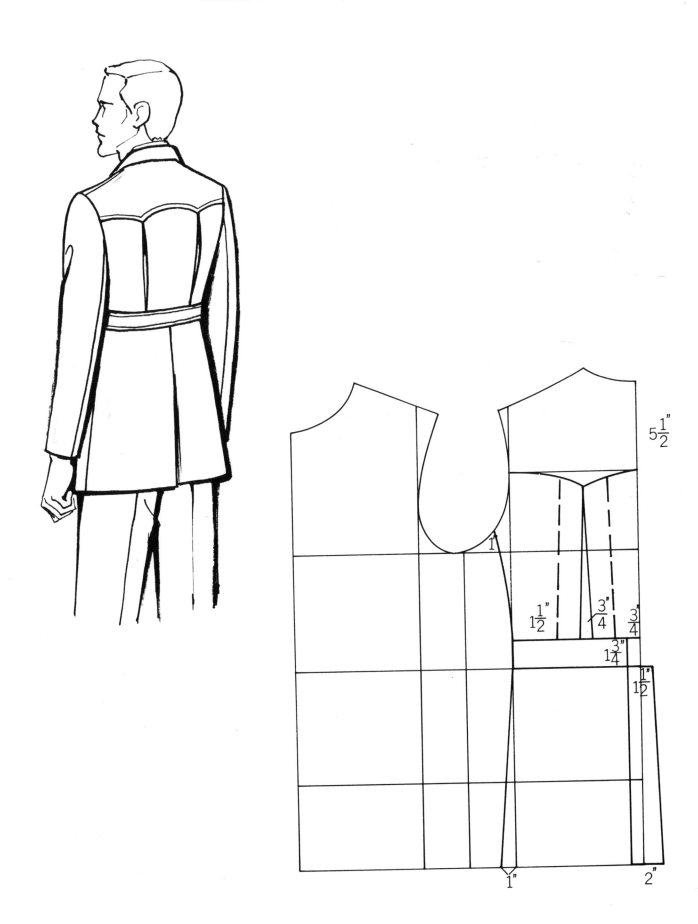

JACKET BACK VIEW, YOKE VARIATION

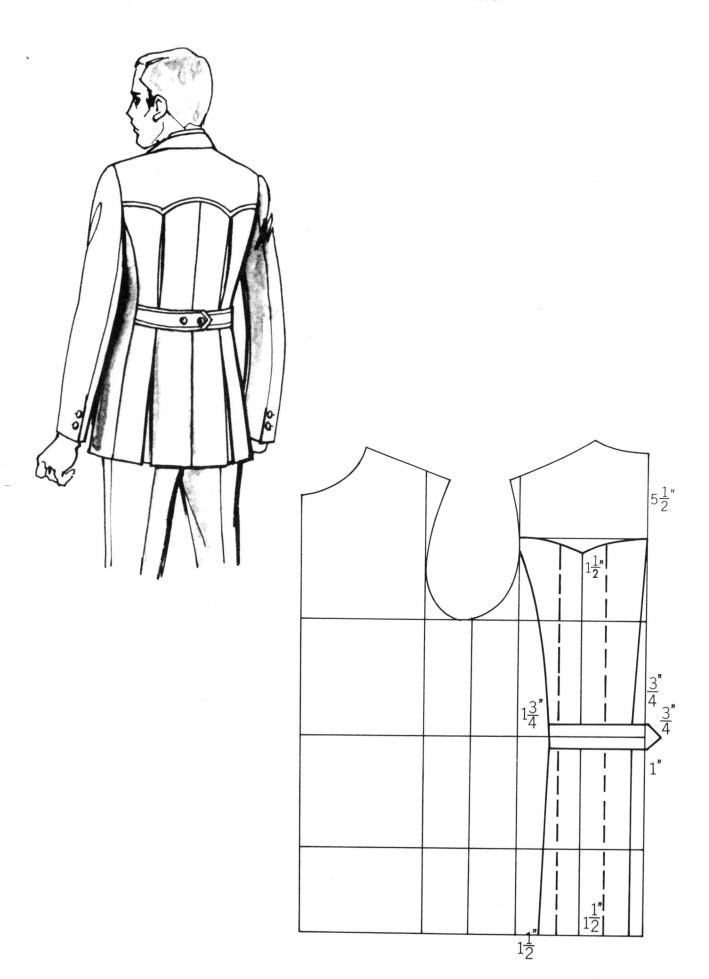

209

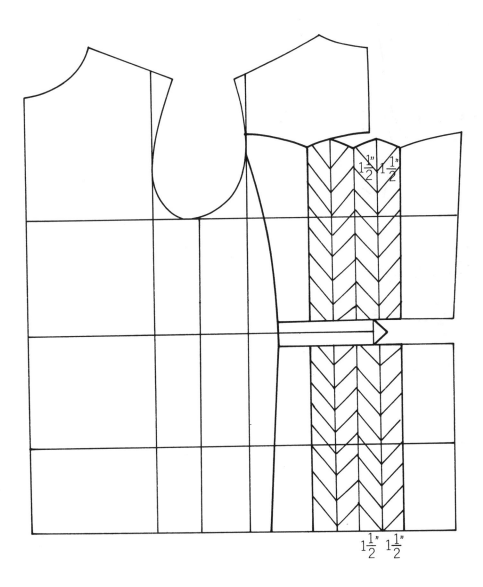

DIAGRAM—Jacket Back View York Variation

JACKET BACK VIEW, SET-IN BELT WITH PLEAT VARIATION

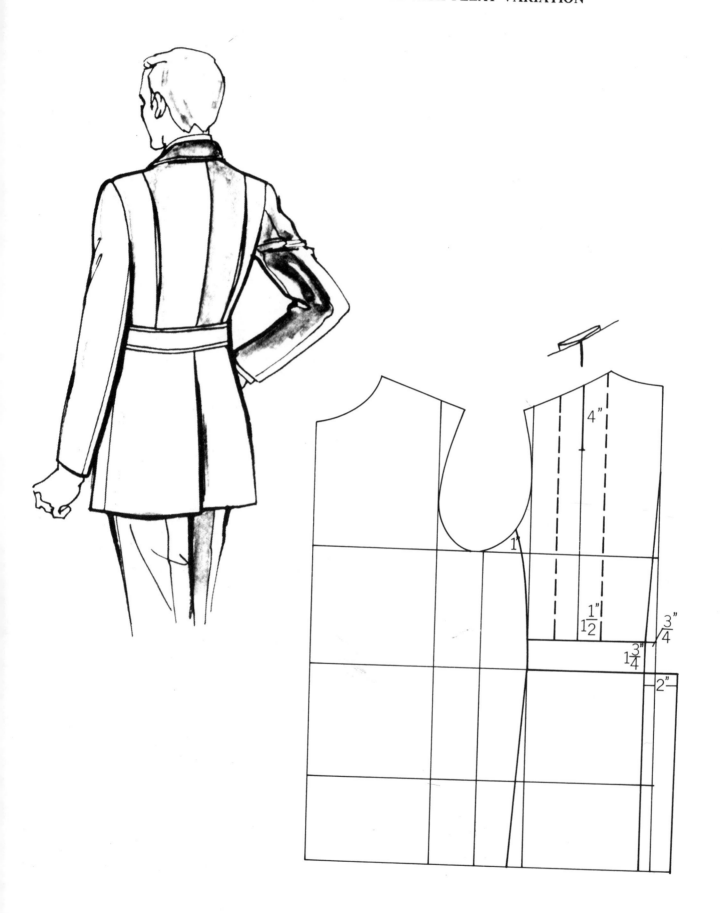

DIAGRAM—Jacket Back View, Set-in Belt with Pleat Variation .

$1\frac{1}{2}''$ $1\frac{1}{2}''$

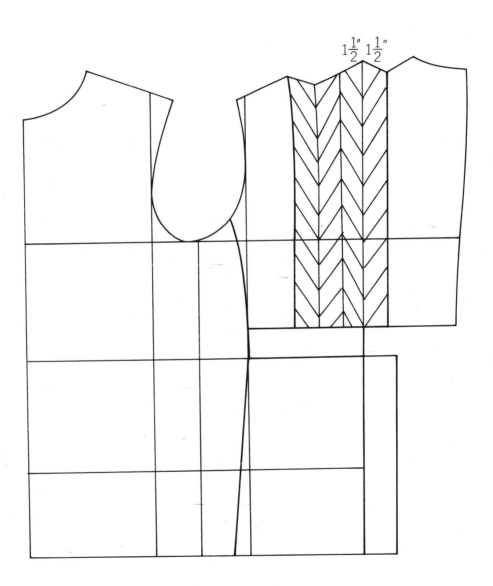

JACKET BACK VIEW, SET-IN BELT WITH PLEAT VARIATION

NOTES

BASIC VEST

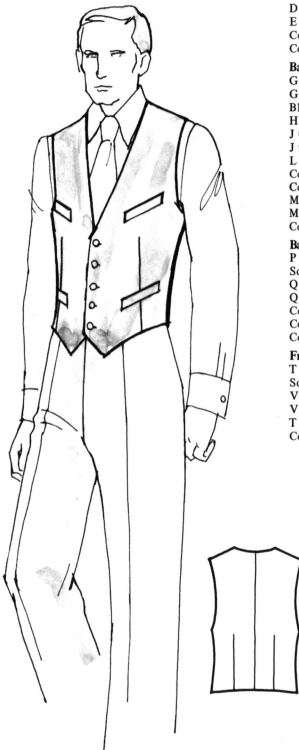

Outline basic sloper and drop waistline 1".

Back Vest Panel
A = 1/4 of neck to chest.
B to C = 1".
D = waist.
D to E = 1" drop.
E to F = 1-1/2".
Connect A to C with shallowest part of hip curve ruler.
Connect C to F with hip curve ruler (see diagram).

Back Shoulder and Armhole
G = shoulder at neckline.
G to H = add 1/4".
Blend H to original neckline.
H to I = 4".
J = side seam at armhole.
J to K = 1".
L = back side guide line.
Connect I to L with sleigh curve ruler.
Connect L to K with sleigh curve ruler to finish back armhole.
M to N = 5/8".
M to O = 1/4".
Connect K to O with hip curve ruler to finish side seam (see diagram).

Back Waist Dart
P = 1/3 of C to L.
Square down P to Q.
Q to R = 1/2".
Q to S = 1/2".
Connect P to R with hip curve ruler.
Connect P to S with hip curve ruler to finish dart.
Connect O to R to finish back vest panel.

Front Vest Panel
T = 1/2 of J to U.
Square down from T to V.
V to W = M to N.
V to X = 1/4".
T to I = 1".
Connect Y to X using same curve as K to O.

Front Shoulder and Armhole
Z = shoulder at neckline.
Z to 1 = add 1/4".
1 to 2 = H to I.
3 = 1/4 of 4 to U.
Connect 2 to 3 with sleigh curve ruler.
Connect 3 to Y with sleigh curve ruler to finish front armhole.
5 = center front at chest.
5 to 6 = 1".
6 to 7 = 1/2" for extension.
Connect 1 to 7 with hip curve ruler to finish neck.
Square down 7 to 8.
8 to 9 = 3-1/2".
9 to 10 = 1-1/2".
11 to 8 = 1".
Connect 11 to 10.
Connect 10 to X with hip curve ruler.

Front Waist Dart
12 = 1/2 of 10 to X.
Connect 4 to 12 with straight guide line.
4 to 13 = 1-1/2".
12 to 14 = 1/2".
12 to 15 = 1/2".
Connect 13 to 14 with hip curve ruler.
Connect 13 to 15 with hip curve ruler to finish front vest.

215

DIAGRAM—Basic Vest

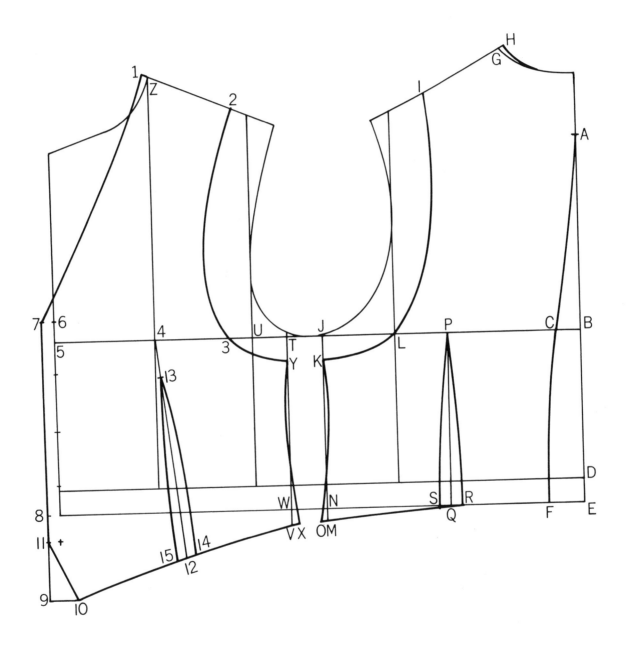

The different collar designs of the jacket can also be
applied to vest designs.

FORMAL VEST WITH SHAWL COLLAR

This particular vest can be adjusted to three different sizes at the back neckband. Elastic is used in the back waistband.

Outline basic sloper.

A to B = 1-1/4".
C to D = add 1/4".
D to E = 2-1/2".
Blend in D to A to finish neckline.
Connect E to B with sleigh curve ruler.
A to F = 1-1/2".
B to G = 1-1/2".
H = 1/2 of F to G.
H to I = 1/2".
Connect F to I.
Connect G to I to finish neck band.

Front Vest Panel
J = shoulder at neckline.
J to K = add 1/4".
K to L = D to E.
M = front side guideline.
N = 1/2 of O to M.
Square down from N to P.
P to Q = 1/3 of P to N.
Q to R = 1/2".
Connect L to M to R with hip curve ruler.
Square down R to S for 1/2".
P to T = 1/2".
Connect S to T.
Square off from R and S toward right for elastic band.
U = center front of waist.
U to V = 2 1/2".
V to W = 1/4".
Square down W to X.
X to Y = 2-1/2".
Y to Z = 1-3/4".
Connect X to Z.
Connect Z to T with hip curve ruler.
Connect K to W with hip curve ruler to finish neckline.

Front Dart
1 = 3/4" from 2.
Square down from 1 to 3.
1 to 4 = 2".
3 to 5 = 3/4".
Connect 4 to 5 with hip curve ruler to finish front dart.

Draw shawl collar outline according to your design.
Note: The shawl collar is a separate piece.

Back Neck Section
(See diagram.)

Note: Back waistband is to be made of elastic.

DIAGRAM–Formal Vest with Shawl Collar

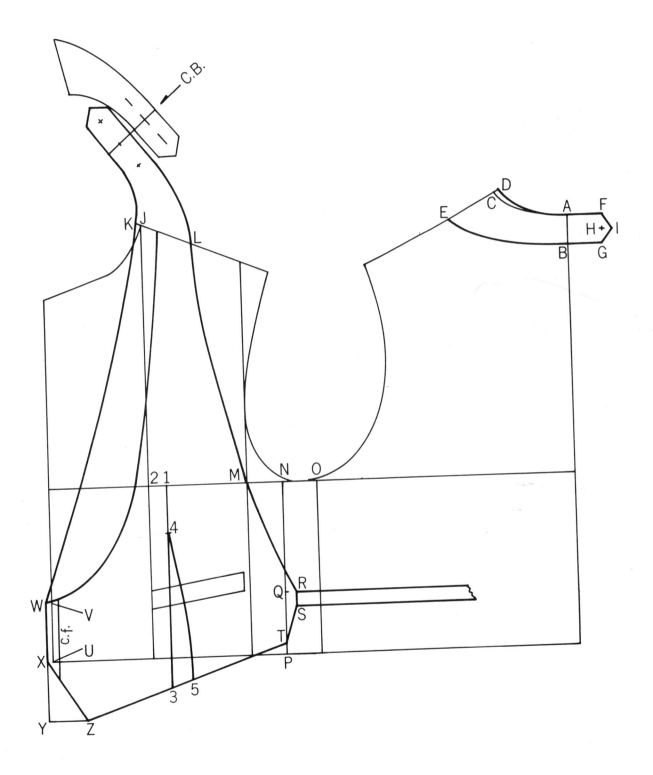

The different collar designs of the jacket can also be applied to vest designs.

ABOUT THE AUTHOR

Born in Japan, Masaaki Kawashima, fashion designer, teacher, author has lived and worked in two countries, the United States and Japan, for the past twenty years. He has created original designs for men and women and made clothes for each. In addition to the present book, he is the author of two widely used basic texts, one in Japanese, *A Standard Text of Pattern Grading* (Bunka School of Fashion Press, 3rd Printing, Tokyo, 1972), and *Men's Outerwear Design* (Fairchild 1977). Presently, he is Associate Professor of Fashion Design at the Fashion Institute of Technology in New York City and Consulting Professor of Fashion Design at the Bunka School of Fashion in Tokyo and the Chiyo Tanaka School of Fashion in Tokyo and Ashiya. In this latter capacity, he has conducted annual seminars for professional designers and manufacturers in the fashion field; these seminars have been the source of many contemporary fashion trends in Japan. Mr. Kawashima serves as Chief Designer and Fashion Consultant for one of the leading Japanese department stores.

Uniquely, he combines the training, talent, experience, and understanding of western ways in fashion with design techniques of Japan.